Think
America
Great

Think America Great

QUICK TRUTHS FOR POLITICAL POP CULTURE

Janie Johnson
Champion of Lemonade Stands

RTR press

Minden, Nevada

RTR Press
Minden, Nevada
RTRPress@gmail.com
www.jjauthor.com

Author website: www.jjauthor.com
Author email: jjauthor@gmail.com

Printed in the United States of America

ISBN Paperback Version: 978-0-9848819-6-3
ISBN eBook Version: 978-0-9848819-7-0

Book Cover & Interior Design: Ghislain Viau

To Ray

Contents

Preface

This book reflects the influences that tweeting has had on America and its capacity to communicate one-on-one with people around the world. So much so, that my thoughts and commentary that reach over 20 million monthly were ranked by MIT as the 105th social media influencer for the 2016 presidential election. Everyday Americans want their voices heard, want the truth, and are not alone in this fight of keeping America great. However, the left does not want my voice and other conservative voices heard.

Twitter not only censors President Donald Trump but nearly all conservatives. Twitter allows Hamas and ISIS and other terrorist groups free rein. Twitter shadowbans (an algorithm that hides and mutes tweets), deletes retweets and tweets, suspends accounts over what it believes are sensitive or hateful comments, and deletes followers. Twitter's latest tactic is to put accounts into a password reset loop. Twitter freezes accounts over unusual activity, makes users reset their passwords, and then doesn't recognize the users' emails or phone numbers. These technical glitches lock users out of their accounts.

This lockout happened to me for over fifty days with thousands of followers lost. Twitter also suspended my account on primary election day and during the State of the Union address. Twitter searches to find an offensive tweet and suspends the account. My guilty offense was wanting to ban Sharia law in the United States by informing everyone of its insidious nature. The left doth protest too. We must take a stand for America and against the mobs cancel culture.

It is freedom of speech that makes America great. We, the people, must think America great!

The world seems upside down presently with COVID-19. We do know never to trust the Communist Chinese. President Trump was 100 percent right to ban China travel early in this pandemic. We need from our government leaders consistent and accurate information on how best to traverse these uncertain times. We must protect our elderly and remember that over 1,600,000 have recovered from the coronavirus. We must stop putting off preventive screenings and services, which will create worse health crises and cancer cases.

We must remain open and refuse lockdowns while taking greater safety precautions, using social distancing, and keeping proper hygiene. The American Academy of Pediatrics and studies from Iceland and Germany agree we must open our schools. We must be informed. We do not need to turn America into China.

We need to think for ourselves. When is the last time you trusted the government on anything?

Since 2010, when I wrote my first book, *Don't Take My Lemonade Stand: An American Philosophy*, I have become dedicated to engaging in the politics of life and government. My goal in writing *Don't Take My Lemonade Stand* was to remind parents, citizens, and patriots why America is exceptional and then teach our kids to keep it exceptional. I found out that was not enough. We must win the war of ideas—the assault on America that is happening in our schools, our media, and our government. Thus, we must think America great.

In my book, *Uncommon Sense: Ammunition for Winning the Culture War*, I wrote an introductory sampling of twenty subjects with twenty truths to give Americans the words to win the war on American greatness. The left often provides well-sounding talking points that undermine American values, and even worse—its lies just don't work! In the Think America Great series of books, I help readers develop their own principles, ideas, and words to fight the insanity of the left. The purpose of principles is to help organize thought, and the purpose of organized thought is to inform actions.

My goal in writing *Don't Take My Lemonade Stand* began as an attempt to answer my then-ten-year-old son Sammy's question, "How do you know who to vote for?" During the writing process, I realized that answering Sammy was harder than it appeared, plus there were many others who needed education on this matter. In particular, I realized that parents and children from all walks of life needed to understand more about the founding of our country, the workings of our politics, and the principles on which our founders relied.

Don't Take My Lemonade Stand became a tutorial for parents, kids, and others to better understand why our country began as it did and has become what it is. During the process of promoting *Don't Take My Lemonade Stand*, I learned much from TV appearances with Sean Hannity, David Asman, *Fox & Friends*, and my local *Nevada Newsmakers*. My radio interviews with Lars Larson, Monica Crowley, and others also proved enlightening. Along the way, I made countless speeches to conservative groups and even appeared on National Public Radio.

With endorsements from Steve Forbes, Lou Holtz, David Asman, David Limbaugh, and others, I found many people loved my book and my message. But worse I found, America and our values were under assault by leftists everywhere!

During my Twitter experience, I offered a few mock Obama 2012 slogans designed to expose the Obama philosophy and contrast it with mine. After a short time, my tweeters asked that I put these slogans into a book. My second book, *Obama 2012 Slogans Rewritten*, made history.

If you believe in an unending cycle of government dependency and wasteful spending or if you are antibusiness or antimilitary—you are on the team I oppose. If you believe in personal responsibility, limited government, free market capitalism, and a strong national defense—we are on the same team.

Please enjoy this first book in my six-book series of Think America Great (TAG), a series of thought-provoking, conservative solutions. TAG, filled with pithy and biting wisdom, is the ammunition that everyday Americans must have to think and express America's winning conservative solutions to fight liberals and to defend and promote the American way!

Coming Soon in the
Think America Great Series

Pray. Vote. Buy a Gun. Conservative Solutions—What Works!

Triggered Truths. Liberals Are Not Liberal

*Democrat Slogans—The Names May Change
but the Slogans Remain the Same*

2020 Campaign Ground Rules—Fake News Rules

*The Cheese Is NOT Free—and Other
Lies the Government Tells You*

I can be found on Twitter @jjauthor.

My website is www.jjauthor.com.

My books are available online.

Happy reading,
Janie Johnson

About the Author

Janie Johnson
Website: www.jjauthor.com
Twitter: @jjauthor
Instagram: jjauthor
Facebook: Janie Johnson
Books:
> *Don't Take My Lemonade Stand: An American Philosophy*
> *Obama 2012 Slogans Rewritten*
> *Uncommon Sense: Ammunition for Winning the Culture War*

Janie wrote her first book, the number one Amazon politics bestseller, *Don't Take My Lemonade Stand: An American Philosophy*, when her then ten-year-old son asked her, "How do you know who to vote for?" She answered, "Whoever makes the government smaller." And only a child could ask, "Why?" It has been Janie's driving force to help everyone to be reminded why everyday citizens must think and educate themselves on why voting matters. Why conservatism with optimism and patriotism will make and keep America great.

Since the release of her first book in 2010, Janie has continued to be a proven conservative influence and was ranked 105 on Who's Influencing Election 2016?—MIT MEDIA LAB—Medium.com. Janie was in the top 50 on the winning side and ahead of Senator Elizabeth Warren and the Democratic National Convention. Her tweets/thoughts/points make a difference!

Janie is a fierce defender of lemonade stands and free markets. She believes everyday people must and can make a difference in how we are governed. If everyday citizens do not stand up to big government shenanigans, who will?

Furthermore, Janie has never given up nor met an obstacle she did not want to overcome. As the youngest of nine kids, she became the number one junior tennis player in the US at age eighteen, a three-time All American at the University of California—Los Angeles (UCLA), Pac Ten Singles Champion, and a top 100 tennis professional while participating in all four Grand Slam tennis tournaments (Wimbledon, the French Open, the Australian Open, and the US Open). Her extensive travels around the world, as a professional tennis player, helped to inform her political philosophy.

Janie is a proven success, whether playing tennis, writing books, or trending subjects on Twitter. She has appeared on *Fox & Friends*, *Fox Business*, Hannity, and has participated in over 500 radio and TV interviews. There is a meaningful battle taking place on screens and on the air across the nation, and the unexpected following Janie has developed highlights the need for a strong voice on the right, a woman's voice, a mom's voice. Janie is helping lead the charge, one frustratingly true and provocative idea at a time.

Janie fights daily for every kid's lemonade stands with over 200,000 Twitter followers. She recognizes that it is with great determination that people must never surrender and never apologize. America's kids and the country are depending on people to act. According to Twitter analytics, she influences over eleven million people monthly.

After leaving the professional tennis circuit and earning a degree in English from UCLA, Janie devoted herself to raising her four children and helping them (and others) to believe that everyday people can and must make a difference in our country. Her brand of common sense conservatism focuses on children, patriotism, and optimism. She is an informed voter who cares deeply about America and its founding principles. She represents all those who have not been particularly involved in the political process until recent events.

Though a registered republican, Janie is displeased with nearly all politicians, including many republicans. Her values are consistent with the US Constitution and the notions of the founders of America. Her books are written by an everyday American for everyday Americans. She firmly believes America cannot leave the education of its citizenry to indoctrinated schools and biased media.

Democrat Dictionary

Leftists operate by manipulating feelings. They use euphemisms and misleading nomenclature when the layperson's word is too revealing of the truths. When people in Washington start creating fancy new phrases, instead of using plain English, you know they are doing something they don't want us to understand!

Democrats use the following euphemisms to avoid citizen and congressional scrutiny. Worse, they think we don't know!

Here are some common words the left substitutes for reality.

1. Abortion—A medical procedure for destroying a group of cells coincidentally shaped like a baby.

2. Affirmative action—Hiring or granting scholarships to people based on the color of their skin rather than the content of their character.

1

3. Affordable housing—Rent control and "the projects" (ghettos).

4. Anti-American—Not a communist.

5. Balanced—My way or the highway. Nothing more!

6. Balanced approach—Higher taxes!

7. Balanced approach—Means you pay, but democrat voters don't!

8. Bigot—Republican.

9. Bipartisan—Leftist agenda accepted without complaint.

10. Climate change—We can control global climate with higher taxes and regulation.

11. Compassion—Spending other people's money.

12. Compromise—When the republicans cede a conflict.

13. Continuing resolution—Kick the can down the road. Let our kids deal with it.

14. Controversial—Infuriatingly truthful.

15. Debt—Unlimited free money.

16. Debt ceiling—The new spending floor.

17. Demagogue—A person, especially a political leader, who gains power by arousing prejudices and passions. Synonym: democrat.

18. Disenfranchisement—Requiring proof of identity to vote.

19. Diversity—Too many white people.

20. Economic justice—Socialist redistribution.

21. Embryonic pulsing—Unborn baby's heartbeat.

22. Entitlement—Dependencies used to control populations, redistribute wealth, and the cause of the budget deficit.

23. Environmental justice—Sacrificing prosperity, quality of life, and employment in exchange for useless money-pit environmental programs.

24. EPA—Employment Prevention Agency!

25. Extremists—God-fearing, red-blooded Americans who value inherent rights; anyone who owns a weapon more dangerous than a golf club.

26. Fair—Hurts the rich or helps the poor, or both.

27. Fair share—From each according to his or her ability, to each according to his or her needs. In short, Marxism.

28. Fair share—Marginal tax rates.

29. Feminism—Having a family with a man and children without premarital sex is an evil societal gender institution.

30. Fiscal restraint—Decreasing the rate at which we are accelerating the increase in national debt we are accruing, periodically, over the next eighteen decades.

31. Gender—Social constructs. Pick yours like you pick the color of your socks.

32. Government—The omnipotent guarantor of individual rights as long as you agree and obey with "the agenda."

33. Greed—When you don't want to fork over your own money, *not* when we want to spend it for you.

34. Green New Deal—A plan to lower the global temperature by setting American infrastructure and economy on fire.

35. Gun control laws—Dissident disarmament measures.

36. Indigenous Peoples' Day—White People Bad Day.

37. Islamophobia—The irrational recognition of the dangers of radical Islam.

38. Judicial—Legislative.

39. Justice-involved individual—Convicted felon.

40. Legality—Morality. If it's legal, it must be moral!

41. Limited kinetic operation—War.

42. Living constitution—The founders were old, slave-owning, racist fools and we know better. Let us change it. Pinky swear we will give it back.

43. Living within your means—Ditching average Joe to starve.

44. Lying—Speaking while conservative.

45. Microaggressions—Anything I don't like.

46. Millionaires and billionaires—The devil.

47. Minimum wage—Under no circumstances should workers negotiate their own wages. The more people on unemployment, the better.

48. Moderate—An anchor on this glorious cruise to a progressive America.

49. MSN—Your daily dose of right think.

50. Multiculturalism—The fewer white people, the better!

51. NPR—The ministry of truth.

52. Obamacare—Medicare for all—beta testing.

53. Obstructionist—Dissident.

54. Phony—Accurate.

55. Plausibility—A lie that's been parroted by enough media outlets.

56. Profit—Theft of employees' wages.

57. Progressivism (Liberalism)—This country sucks. Let's change all of it.

58. Quantitative easing—Currency manipulation.

59. Racist—Republican, conservative, any nonleftist.

60. Religious—Bigoted backward hillbilly.

61. Rent control—More homeless people, please.

62. Republican—A right-wing, gun-hoarding, hateful, bigoted Nazi, or an ignorant hick who doesn't know better, or anyone in between.

63. Rich—Greedy.

64. Right—A conditional privilege granted to individuals by the government.

65. Scandal—Republicans did once what democrats do daily.

66. Sequester—No, not spending. *Sequestering.*

67. Smart tax rate—Higher tax rate.

68. Social justice—Reparations.

69. Sustainability—Useless and wildly expensive environmental "renewable energy" programs to nationalize infrastructure and aggregate power.

70. Tax increase—Higher taxes on only the richest people and definitely not the middle class.

71. Tax the rich—Tax employers and job creators.

72. Taxes—Money the government doesn't trust you to spend *correctly.*

73. Tea Party—Terrorists (Yeah, "reporters" actually said that— on national TV).

74. Tolerance—The acceptance of all things different to our own. Except opinions, naturally.

75. Transparency—Controlled leaks.

76. Unaffordable—Anything that cannot be bought with a single, minimum-wage paycheck.

77. Undocumented immigrant—Illegal alien.

78. Unsustainable energy—Coal, natural gas, or nuclear power.

79. White nationalist /Supremacist—Anyone who disagrees with us.

1

The Ministry of Truth

If you don't read the newspaper, you are uninformed.
If you do read the newspaper, you are misinformed.
—Mark Twain

1. When the liberal media say, "Donald Trump is not connecting with ordinary people," how could they know?

2. Could we please stop calling these reporters "journalists"? They are the democrats' palace guards!

3. Democrats have a public relation advantage. Media supports their ruthless lies and the rest of us are limited by the truth!

4. Democrats construct an image of reality, then the media documents it for them!

5. With Google, it seems it matters how we think, not what we did!

6. The media will never focus on the widening gap between democrat promises and democrat deliveries!

7. When a democrat talks, the national media endlessly echoes!

8. Media rules for covering democrats: echo democrats' excuses and never put any democrat in an unflattering light!

9. I forget! Does the Democratic National Committee (DNC) give the fakers at fake news the latest talking points, or does fake news give the democrats the "news"?

10. It seems every "journalist" has become an activist with an agenda!

11. No matter what the media says, the only poll that matters is at the ballot box.

12. The national media "journalists" aren't watchdogs. They're lap dogs.

13. What on earth is the defensible purpose of government radio or TV?

14. Talking points are not facts, no matter how many times they are repeated by politicians or the media!

15. When it comes to conservatives, the leftwing media and politicians consider themselves judge, jury, and executioner!

16. A dutiful and sycophant media member must be called a "gossip columnist!"

17. One thing I learned from the media: the people might be still evaluating the candidates but the pundits have clearly made up their minds!

18. Is it not truly surprising that anyone was actually too foul for the MSNBC television channel?

19. We are the antidotes to much of the nonsense that comes out of the DNC and the press corps!

20. When the national media keeps repeating, "Donald Trump is not one of us," I say, "Thank God!"

21. Who in the media has been asking the right questions? Answer—Very, very few!

2

The Unmelted Pot

I had always hoped that this land might become a safe
& agreeable Asylum to the virtuous & persecuted part
of mankind, to whatever nation they might belong.
—George Washington

1. Wanting a secure border has nothing to do with race.

2. If twelve to twenty-two million new immigrants from Mexico will help the US economy, why didn't they help the Mexican economy before they left?

3. So, apparently we cannot possibly deport a million people, but we seem to have no problem importing a million and setting them up for life.

4. Democrats do not want an immigration overhaul; they want open borders and more democratic voters!

5. When did demanding that people come to this country legally become too much to ask?

6. Stop calling undocumented workers "illegal aliens." They are unregistered democrats!

7. So, if current immigrations laws are mocked and disregarded, what makes us think new ones will be respected?

8. Why do democrats choose illegals over citizens?

9. Without border security first, immigration laws only exist on paper. There is no sovereignty.

10. What kind of danger, damage, or tragedy must occur at the US/Mexico border before Congress will secure it?

11. Imagine Democratic Party outrage if the GOP was importing an undeveloped third world country underclass to create a Republican GOP permanent majority?

12. If illegal immigrants began to vote Republican, the US southern border would be closed within hours!

13. Illegal immigrants won't be happy until they get full amnesty and full welfare rights. Democrats won't be happy until illegals can vote!

14. Open borders do not exist. We either have borders or we do not!

15. The "heat" in our American melting pot is not high enough to assimilate all we are placing in it!

16. If democrats were being honest, their new immigration campaign slogan would be "Save illegal immigration!"

17. Democrats not only gave young illegals deferred deportation, they gave them work permits, free college, healthcare, welfare, housing, electronic benefits transfer (EBT) cards, and driver's licenses!

18. The true solution for resolving the illegal immigrant crisis is to replace those in Congress who will not vote to secure the border!

19. As conservatives, many of us think an immigration deal is simple. Secure the borders—then clean up the legal visa and work permit process!

20. For every sad story that liberals tell about deportations, there are thousands about illegals who commit crimes or live off the US taxpayer!

21. Liberals use the term "undocumented immigrant" to make it sound like no one broke the law!

22. If liberals didn't believe illegal immigrants would vote for democrats, they'd drop them like a hot rock!

23. If everyone who can sneak into America can stay, everyone who can, will!

24. Is there any reason other than the desire to allow illegal immigrants into our country for not wanting to secure the border?

25. Without border security, there can be no material enforcement of immigration laws no matter their content!

26. Democrats don't just give illegals sanctuary, they give them subsidized sanctuary!

27. With "legalization first with no secure border," how many terrorists do democrats want to let into America?

28. If we do not have borders, we are not a country.

29. Politicians need to do what is right for America on immigration instead of their campaigns: border security, track foreigners, and welfare reform!

30. Is there anyone left who believes a democrat supports making illegal immigrants legal for any reason other than political advantage?

3

Vote! Dead or Alive

*I consider it completely unimportant who in the party
will vote, or how; but what is extraordinarily important
is this—who will count the votes, and how.*
—Joseph Stalin

1. Only in America ... could we need to present a driver's
   license to cash a check or buy alcohol, but not to vote.

2. How big an insult is it that liberals believe millions of
   African Americans would find getting a voter identification
   (ID) card too onerous?

3. It is not voter suppression to require an ID. It is voter
   suppression when we allow someone illegal to vote or to
   vote two times or more.

4. It seems a bit hypocritical that unions are against voter IDs
   in US presidential elections but require a picture ID to vote
   in a union election!

5. Why are democrats so against the US upgrading to Mexican voter ID standards?

6. Voter ID suppresses voters! It suppresses the illegal, dead, and multiple voters.

7. There is finally conclusive evidence that Osama bin Laden, Sulieman, and Muammar Gaddafi are dead. They are all registered to vote in Chicago.

8. What democrats mean when they are promoting ease of access is to vote early and vote often!

9. By law, you have to show a photo ID to buy decongestants but not to vote.

10. What is it that liberals have against honest elections?

11. Photo IDs only suppress *ILLEGAL* votes!

12. The democrats in government still consider "voter fraud" a voting right!

13. It has to be asked. Are people who are not smart enough to get an ID democrats, or are democrats just not smart enough to get an ID?

14. Photo ID votes make it easy to see which political party thinks it benefits from voter fraud!

15. Is the government suppressing welfare by requiring an ID? If so, it must be really bad at it!

16. Who do you know that is so limited in intellect or resources that they cannot get a free government ID?

17. Not having a voter ID does not stop anyone from voting. A provisional ballot is given and counted once and verified!

18. African American thugs outside a voting site are not voter intimidation but voter IDs are! Liberal justice!

19. Will it take a picture ID to get into the Democratic National Convention? My guess is it will!

20. Progressives don't fear that any American citizens will have trouble getting voter IDs; they fear that illegals will have difficulty getting them!

21. Why are the democrats so fearful of voter ID requirements? I think we know!

22. Cynical liberals are still against states making voters prove who they say they are with a free voter ID!

23. The anti-voter ID movement has one primary objective: allow illegals to vote!

24. Democrats still insist they oppose proof of citizenship and voter ID solely to protect legal voting. Really?

25. Liberals still find it unreasonable that voters are required to be who they are—and only one time for each election!

26. Don't you "love" the liberal argument that voting fraud is rare, so let's not stop it? What crap! Voter IDs won't stop anyone but illegals!

27. Isn't it the liberals who imply that poor and minority people are too stupid to get picture IDs?

4

The Two-Income Death Trap—Jobs

The best social program is a job.
—**Ronald Reagan**

1. Is it possible democrats would rather see Americans unemployed and in need of government assistance?

2. Have you noticed that democrats seem to want to work on just about any liberal cause, as long as it does not include jobs for Americans!

3. Once again, America needs jobs, but Joe Biden is campaigning on useless gun control and giving more preapproved speeches from his basement.

4. Although we need jobs, Biden needs campaign issues and political tension. That's been his whole life!

5. Democrats want to "dig" in free contraceptives, abortion protection, climate change, immigration—everything but jobs and national security!

6. Did Biden really say his infrastructure plan would address needed jobs now? Has any democrat ever tried to build anything in the US? Environmental impact reports, assessments, and impact statements take years.

7. If Biden wanted to enhance his "jobs plan," he could eliminate capital gains and repatriation taxes and allow 100 percent first-year depreciation. But he won't!

8. Biden's "jobs plan" will likely just be a speech that touts making buildings "green," funding schools, subsidizing certain mortgages, and spending—for democrat donors only!

9. Jobless benefits might or might not need to be extended, but they certainly need to be reformed to include work and training!

10. So, if the government can claim that those not currently looking for a job are no longer considered unemployed, unemployment seems to improve!

11. Is unemployment really being "reduced" by people getting so discouraged they quit looking for work or take a fast food job? Not!

12. Now that we know "freeing people from work" is a liberal objective, perhaps we better understand their many programs!

13. If government spending created jobs, we would all be working!

14. If we want job creation, we need innovation. And if we want innovation, we need to put capital at risk. This could not be simpler.

15. Perhaps a democrat doesn't realize that assigning blame for unemployment is not the same as creating jobs!

16. Under Trump, there is the lowest unemployment rate in fifty years: 3.5 percent!

17. Only a democrat would forgo a job in lieu of benefits.

18. Democrats still want us to subsidize other people's choice to work less or not work at all!

19. The problem in job creation is not "uncertainty." It is the "certainty" that the democrats will institute the wrong policies!

20. No individual can make better economic decisions than a free market.

21. Democrats' economists seem to see joblessness as a "choice" to be encouraged, not a problem to be solved!

22. Have you noticed that the "official" unemployment number seems to have little to do with actual full-time employment?

23. The government does not create any net additional jobs. The government is *not* the solution and oftentimes exacerbates the job market.

24. Is there any logical reason, except political expediency, for not counting certain unemployed people as unemployed?

25. Crooks' adjustments of their economic metrics sounds painfully like the way our government calculates unemployment!

26. First, our government statistically subtracts people from the workforce if they have not actively looked for work in the past four weeks.

27. How does not actively looking for work in the past four weeks make a person who needs a job, but doesn't have one, less unemployed?

28. Next our government has some sort of "black box" calculation that makes seasonal adjustments to the real unemployment number.

29. Then our government loosens the definition of disabled, so people who are stressed about not working count as disabled, not unemployed!

30. The media then hypes or hates (depending on a Republican or Democrat White House) the top line "adjusted" unemployment number (say 8.3 percent) and deemphasizes the number of disabled, dropped out, or underemployed! Rigged!

31. Joe Biden's rhetoric is pro-jobs but his actions are anti-job creators. Is there any way this can make sense?

32. The problem in job creation is not uncertainty—it is the certainty that Biden will institute the wrong policies!

33. It seems as if the democrats are passionate about nearly anything as long as it is *not* jobs, the debt, the economy, or the deficit!

34. Now, democrats tell us that having some pay for the "right" of others not to work is a good thing!

35. How many of the unemployed are those who can't work or can't find work, versus those unemployed who just won't work?

36. Who in the government decided the long-term unemployed were so discouraged we shouldn't even count them as unemployed?

37. Democrats' solution to unemployment/underemployment is to raise taxes, to increase regulations, and to stop enforcing immigration laws!

38. Liberals restrict growth but support new jobs. Go figure!

39. How many workers has a democrat helped get to the unemployment line, and how many have they enabled to stay there?

5

The Climate Apocalypse

Science, however, is never conducted as a popularity contest, but instead advances through testable, reproducible, and falsifiable theories.
—Michio Kaku

1. The only "science" related to climate change is political $cience!

2. The only thing climate change is a threat to is science!

3. How much global warming alarmist hot air must we tolerate with grace?

4. The question isn't if human-made climate change exists (not likely), it's whether anything democrats are planning would make a difference!

5. Is it more foolish to believe in "climate change" or "climate control"?

6. When will climate change alarmists take to China and India for their overwhelming share of carbon emissions?

7. Is the "heat" caused by global warming, or does global warming cause the "cold"?

8. It's telling that socialists and communists are drawn to environmentalism.

9. What climate alarmists want most is fewer people. They each have one life to give to that plan!

10. These state and federal environmental studies often take years to complete. They are then often followed by environmental lawsuits!

11. So-called environmentalists abuse envirostudies and the Endangered Species Act to stall, hoping developers will run out of resources!

12. The word "alternative," as in alternative energy, is a euphemism for an "unproven" and "uneconomical" vote-buying scam!

13. Have you ever wondered why all the special clean air rules adopted in California have not cleaned up the smog and pollution?

14. If it rains—global warming. If it's dry—global warming. If it's cold—weather. If there's a storm—global warming!

15. If the world were ending in ten years, why bother saving money, voting, having kids, etc?

16. What the warming alarmists have proved is that scientists can make a computer model say whatever they want it to.

17. Global warming was masterfully propagated by the issuance of "research" grants to give this scam the appearance of legitimacy!

18. One wonders how many of the people buying into this carbon credit scam are con artists versus just gullible.

19. The true goal of environmentalism is the elimination of capitalism and modernity!

20. For liberals, it's never been about climate change, it's been about climate change taxes!

21. Democrats will focus on their climate change hoax. Their other hoaxes have been largely exposed!

22. There are few, if any, climate prophets forecasting doom who are not profiting from their prognostications!

23. Global warming was always a political tool to give government more control over individuals!

24. Everyone is against pollution, however, liberals abuse environmental laws and regulations to delay or eliminate any human development!

25. If liberals had their way, every species, except people, would be legally proclaimed to be an endangered species!

26. It seems environmental wackos like everything about nature—except people!

27. Once again, liberals are satisfied with what sounds good rather than what works. That's even if we buy into their global warming scam!

6

Shut Up and Get Canceled

If . . . the freedom of Speech may be taken away—and,
dumb & silent we may be led, like sheep, to the Slaughter.
—George Washington

1. Let the First Amendment be the speech code!

2. Who decides what constitutes "hate speech"?

3. To many liberals, most of what the US Constitution says is a "thought crime!"

4. When universities establish "free speech zones," does that imply that all other zones are censored speech zones?

5. Apparently, First Amendment rights of free speech stop at university boundaries.

6. We live in a free country, not some communist dictatorship or college campus. Censorship is not an option!

7. Apparently, democrats' answer to any argument is to "Shut the hell up or get cancelled!"

8. No democrat ever vigorously, or even limply, defends the right of free speech.

9. Everything progressives say about protecting "free speech" and "diversity" is a lie. They don't want free speech or diversity.

10. Constitutionally protected free speech appears crass to those who abhor the notion of unabashed individual freedom.

11. Democrats don't burn books in America. They now rewrite or ban them.

12. Word that best summarizes political correctness— censorship!

13. Don't forget the golden rule of big tech: never make the mistake of having an opinion while conservative.

14. If you believe that freedom of speech is fine as long as nobody is offended by it, you might be a democrat.

15. The campus free speech movements of the past have morphed into thought control forums.

16. "We'll defend our constitutional rights of speech, and assembly, and religion" has never been said by a democrat.

17. Constitutionally protected free speech appears crass to those who oppose your speech.

18. The truth is not necessary for the left to demonize an opponent or champion an idea!

19. When did all these US mayors rip up the US Constitution and decide they had to power to limit the Chick-fil-A owners' or any other business owners' free speech?

20. The real question is whether Twitter and other social media platforms must follow the laws of the countries they are in or must they fight for nearly unlimited free speech?

7

It's Okay to Be White

I look to a day when people will not be judged by the color of their skin, but by the content of their character.
—Martin Luther King Jr.

1. When is the time for the nation to finally put affirmative action preferences and all forms of discrimination behind it?

2. Race only matters to racists.

3. Republicans have never elected a Ku Klux Klan majority leader!

4. A racist is anyone who wins an argument with a democrat.

5. Race-baiters often show their racist tendencies when they call others "racists!"

6. Because liberals think Asians are bright and Caucasians are privileged, what do they think about African Americans and Hispanics?

7. The *only* way to stop discrimination on the basis of race is to stop discriminating on the basis of race.

8. It appears race hustlers want to be judged on the color of their skin, *not* on the content of their character!

9. It's racist to call others racist just because they disagree with you!

10. Democrats don't support African Americans and other minorities. They use them!

11. Race-baiters make their living fanning the flames of envy and hatred!

12. The white privilege movement is a pitch against capitalism and for the welfare state!

13. Why do all the professional race hustlers congregate in the Democratic Party?

14. Liberals keep complaining about so-called "racist dog whistles" and they do so incessantly!

15. The people who react to the whistle always assume it's intended for somebody else!

16. The whole point of the dog whistle metaphor is that if you can hear the whistle, you're the dog!

17. Race hustling is a thriving industry!

18. Where is the race hustler or grievance industry exploiter who asks to be judged by the content of his or her character?

19. Have you noticed any word is a code word for racist—community, neighborhood, poor—when your only lens is racist!

20. There is no more talk of a "post-racial" nation because the notion was only a liberal talking point with no intent or substance!

21. Race hustlers and the grievance industry often reserve rhetorical prerogatives for themselves that they deny others!

22. There are too many cases where the term "civil rights" has become synonymous with the notion of "grievance industry exploiter!"

23. The one thing Al Sharpton and Jesse Jackson do *not* want is to be judged by the content of their characters!

24. Democrats believe in using race-based discrimination to overcome race-based discrimination!

25. The prime question about affirmative action is should our government use current discrimination to rectify past discrimination?

26. Being a black conservative just doesn't fit the liberal narrative!

27. Are democrats seeking justice for what they see as "social justice"?

28. How many political thumbs are now pressing on the scales of justice in the police shooting investigations?

29. Looting was never a legitimate part of peaceful protest!

30. I am not a racist because I do not like Barack Obama's policies! I don't like Joe Biden or Nancy Pelosi's policies either! I love Dr. Thomas Sowell, Dr. Walter Williams, and Dr. Larry Elder!

8

Shall Not Be Infringed

No free man shall ever be debarred the use of arms.
—Thomas Jefferson

1. There is no gun control debate. The Second Amendment exists and some fools want it not to!

2. Gun control is not about guns. It is all about control!

3. Why is it that liberals so want to disarm the population?

4. When an organization or a government entity bans guns, they in effect ban self-defense!

5. In Nevada, there is a gun registry—it's called a phone book!

6. Gun control laws cannot stop criminals from getting guns. Laws don't stop criminals!

7. Being stripped of the ability to defend yourself makes you "safer," according to the government—liberal nonsense!

8. One thing for sure, successfully banning private gun ownership will leave nearly all the guns in the hands of criminals!

9. As with gun control, support for immigration reform requires that which is in short supply—trust in the government!

10. It should be illegal for democrats to own guns. Take the guns from democrats and we've just reduced gun crime by about 97 percent!

11. Liberals constantly decry the power of the National Rifle Association (NRA), but what's really bothering them is the Second Amendment and the power of the American people!

12. The only gun rights we have in this world . . . are the ones we are willing to fight for!

13. This is my gun permit—the Second Amendment!

14. Liberals tell us not to judge all Muslims by the actions of a few lunatics. However, they judge all gun owners by the actions of a few loons—liberal hypocrisy!

15. If you believe in Second Amendment rights, don't vote for a democrat. It's that simple!

16. Picture America with no strong defense, no armed citizenry, no guns, and no police—democrats do!

17. Progressive Commandment: Criminals don't kill people. Law-abiding citizens with guns kill people!

18. Progressive Commandment: Criminals need short sentences and cushy jails to rehabilitate them!

19. Operation Choke Point's goal was to stop banking services for gun companies. The democrats want your guns!

20. Was Operation Fast and Furious an illegal gunrunning operation or just an "undocumented" gunrunning operation?

9

PhDs for Plumbers

The philosophy of the school room in one generation will be the philosophy of government in the next.
—Abraham Lincoln

1. Failing public schools—liberals built that!

2. Is the government even capable of improving education? Does the government even want to?

3. Failing unaffordable colleges—liberals built that!

4. When rich liberals send their kids to private schools, do they first check for "adequate" diversity?

5. Has the US Department of Education actually educated anyone?

6. When we eliminate the entire Department of Education, we will not be cutting education. It does not educate anyone!

7. When liberals ruined our school systems—they were on the wrong side of history!

8. How related is the deterioration of US education and the establishment of the Department of Education bureaucracy?

9. If we don't measure teacher performance, we won't manage it. If we don't manage teacher performance, it will get worse!

10. How long should we leave an issue as important as educating our youth in the hands of an incompetent government?

11. If the poorly educated entertainment industry can figure out how to pay the best performers the most, why can't highly educated teachers?

12. Liberals oppose school vouchers because they put teachers' union political contributions ahead of educating minority children!

13. What teachers and other public employees give up to protect poor performers is a reward for good performers!

14. Who would be fighting school choice if members of Congress and government officials were required to send their kids to public schools?

15. Democrats continue to sacrifice the education of poor and minority children to the interests of the teachers' unions and the democrats' union dues!

16. Liberals oppose school vouchers because they want unions to have school choice, not parents!

17. Our educational system has let us down. Instead of teaching the skills to take risks and start a business, it focuses on social justice

18. Democrats' union education plan is simple: if the kids can't pass the test, either lower the standard for passing or quit giving the test!

19. Student achievement is nowhere in the teacher evaluation process—so kids can fail while the teachers succeed!

20. Teachers are important, but there is never a time when taking care of teachers is more important than taking care of kids!

21. Liberals fail to notice that past increases in education spending have not resulted in improved education. The money has not been well spent!

22. We must remind ourselves why America is great and teach our kids to keep it that way!

10

Remember the Crusades

My concern is not whether God is on our side; my greatest concern is to be on God's side, for God is always right.
—Abraham Lincoln

1. The official motto of the United States is "In God We Trust."

2. It's freedom *of* religion, not freedom *from* religion. Tell a liberal!

3. When democrats see a cross, they see intolerance and bigotry, and Christians will be treated as such.

4. The only celebrities who won't be mocked for attending church are politicians. Would they be going on their own?

5. Religious freedom does not end at small businesses. Forcing someone to violate the tenets of their religion is why people left Europe.

6. Do liberals reject "religious values" because they don't agree with the values or because they don't like the notion of religion?

7. The Democratic Party omitted all references to God in its platform. Is there any chance this was just an oversight?

8. Why are there no mounting protests by the so-called moderate Muslims condemning and excommunicating radical terrorists?

9. The left denies our Judeo-Christian founding and insists that humans produce objective morality. Objective morality like abortion?

10. Liberals stepped up their war on religion when they made it illegal to pray in school!

11. It's odd the people who don't believe in God seem to be experts on the Bible.

12. Who are the nimrods that believe a "war on Christmas" even needs to be fought? What could they possibly hope to win?

13. Teach a man to fish and he'll eat for life. Give a man someone else's fish and he'll vote for you!

14. Muslim brotherhood says that "Allah is our objective, the Prophet is our leader; the Quran is our law; dying in the way of Allah is our highest hope."

15. Islam is misunderstood to be violent and Christianity is misunderstood to be peaceful, if the left is to be believed.

16. Are there really some sensitive souls who feel coerced merely by being in the presence of public prayers? Can we get them help?

17. Why do democrats openly hate only the Judeo-Christian God?

18. One wonders when the democrats will tell the Muslims to stop clinging to their guns and religion.

19. I am proud to be a bitter clinger!

20. Only secular Jews vote blue. Why?

21. Church tax exemption *will* be attacked under the guise of lesbian, gay, bisexual, transgender, or queer (LGBTQ) activism.

11

Entitled-ments

*Those who would give up essential Liberty, to purchase a
little temporary Safety, deserve neither Liberty nor Safety.*
—Benjamin Franklin

1. The entitlement train is rolling, the track is ending, and
    liberals are calling for more speed!

2. We gave the government a Social Security trust fund. It
    took the money and spent it—not on Social Security!

3. Social Security is a Ponzi scheme and a great big lie!

4. The 1936 government pamphlet on Social Security said,
    "That is the most you will ever pay." Said before rates were
    raised!

5. You have no property right at all to your Social Security
    contributions! *None!*

6. Americans were sold on the belief that Social Security is like a retirement account and money placed in it is their property.

7. Congress attempts to dupe Americans when it phonies up its accounting and when it "creatively" names a new piece of legislation!

8. Government's future commitments to Social Security, Medicare, etc., do *not* appear on Uncle Sam's balance sheet.

9. Think about the term entitlement. If Americans are entitled to something they didn't earn, where does Congress get the money?

10. Entitlement is a left-wing invention that makes welfare programs sound like constitutional rights.

11. Entitlements are not debts owed. They are confiscations of other people's money expected and demanded!

12. Entitlements are not legitimate debts owed. They are illegitimate political payoffs promised by corrupt politicians!

13. An entitlement is legal theft. Congress forces one American to pay for another American. I thought slavery was outlawed?

14. Politicians need to admit that they spent all the Social Security money and there is none left. There are only Social Security obligations, no cash!

15. Democrats' Obamacare stole 716 billion dollars from Medicare and gave it to Medicaid.

16. Will Congress put forward a plan to reform and save entitlements such as Medicare? Not!

17. Liberals know that Medicare and, to a lesser degree, Social Security are unsustainable, but this is not an issue for them!

18. Democrats, or rather the socialists, want to turn Medicare from an earned benefit to a welfare program. It's just that simple!

19. The Social Security trust fund gave its real money to the US Department of Treasury and accepted electronic vouchers in return!

20. Annual entitlement and mandatory spending (that is, union contracts) equal more than 100 percent of federal tax revenues! No painless solution!

21. All government spending (except payment on government debt) is discretionary. Change is allowed and legal.

22. Oddly, the folks who are getting free stuff don't like the folks paying for the free stuff.

23. The folks who are getting the free stuff are not satisfied with the amount of free stuff they are getting.

24. We have let the free-stuff giving go on for so long, there are now more people getting free stuff than paying for free stuff.

12

Hawk If You Do, Dove If You Don't

Of the four wars in my lifetime, none came about because the US was too strong.
—Ronald Reagan

1. Democrat doctrine is to aid, appease, and abet our enemies; alienate, annoy, and anger our allies!

2. Why is pouring water on a terrorist's head torture, but vaporizing him by remote control drone humane?

3. Politicians need to realize that if they engage in war, that, along with the bad guys, innocents will be killed.

4. Losing wars for political or politically correct reasons is a total misunderstanding of war and the value of life!

5. Only enter a war if it is both winnable and worth winning. Don't enter a war if you are not prepared to win it!

6. Iran is still dedicated to spreading terror, destroying Israel, and dominating the region!

7. Imagine defending Qasem Soleimani.

8. The liberal media would sacrifice the lives of Iranian and Hong Kong protestors to maintain negative coverage of the president.

9. Trump is dropping bombs on our enemies and cash on our allies—while Obama dropped pacifiers and blankies.

10. Appeasement only allows you to be killed—last.

11. Obama funded Iran, and Iran funds terrorism.

12. Trump has been drawing thick red lines over Obama's dotted magenta ones.

13. Iran is not moderate. Period.

14. Abandoning the Middle East will allow threats to our country to fester and grow.

15. Iran is less interested in war than the US, it knows a war would mean complete annihilation.

16. Crushing terrorists is never a bad idea.

17. The military wants to do its job. Don't back out of lifesaving or national security operations on account of the troops. Let them do their jobs.

18. Iranian and Hong Kong protestors are more patriotic than the Democratic Party, which insists America is an imperial force for evil in the world.

19. Why do democrats protect and praise terrorists and punish and criminalize patriots?

20. Don't you think the democrats would dismantle the entire military if they could?

13

Benghazi— Benghazi Ain't Going Away!

If the battle for civilization comes down to the wimps versus the barbarians, the barbarians are going to win.
—Thomas Sowell

1. Is it possible the Benghazi cover-up was done to hide that Americans were being killed with weapons the US provided?

2. If we didn't know how long the Benghazi attack would last, how did we know time was too short to send help?

3. As it turned out, neither Hillary Clinton nor Barack Obama did anything to save those lost in Benghazi!

4. Where were President Obama and Secretary of State Clinton hiding on the night of September 11, 2012?

5. We know the government is hiding nonclassified information from us and purposely misrepresenting costs. Why do we let it continue?

6. What are the odds that the leaking of General David Petraeus's affair was timed to keep him quiet on Benghazi?

7. Who changed the Benghazi talking points to include the protest and the film? Please ask Obama!

8. Why didn't Obama send help to save the ambassador and others who died in Benghazi?

9. Democratic Benghazi deniers evidently believe that lies and cover-ups should just be ignored!

10. Why is it so hard for Obama to answer the simple question, "Who made the decision *not* to send help to Benghazi?"

11. If Hillary didn't know and couldn't find out what happened in Benghazi, why did we need her?

12. One thing we know for sure, Barack and Hillary are hiding something—and it is *not* nothing!

13. Why did Obama silence the Benghazi whistleblowers?

14. Four Americans dead, inadequate consulate protection, false talking points, and hidden witnesses do not sound phony!

15. In Benghazi, there was an extreme failure of character, but integrity had long left the building!

16. Now we know that neither Hillary nor Barack were prepared to take that three A.M. call!

17. Obama and friends only changed the Benghazi talking points twelve times!

18. Lying over a dead ambassador's coffin added severe insult to fatal injury!

19. Never forget Benghazi!

20. Benghazi ain't going away!

14

The Government Spends
It Better—Cut Spending

*For a nation to try to tax itself into prosperity is like a man
standing in a bucket and trying to lift himself up by the handle.*
—Winston Churchill

1. Democrats don't realize that the government doesn't make
    money and can't spend unless it first takes it out of the
    private sector.

2. This "spending more than you make" dilemma seems to
    perplex most of Congress.

3. How many ways do politicians have for arguing against
    "living within our means"?

4. The only way to reduce the overreach of government is to
    reduce the size of government!

5. If the government is not limited by the people, it will expand forever!

6. Is there any chance that democrats and their band of liberals really thinks that every piece of government spending provides an essential service?

7. Government spending is, of course, the primary issue, but it is the one issue Congress will put off until later, and asking Congress to decrease government spending is like asking a dog to quit wagging its tail!

8. Think about it. How hard can it be for members of Congress or a president to remember, "It's the spending, stupid!"

9. Have you noticed how often the concept of "living within your means" is now described as "ruthless austerity"?

10. Every business and every family must figure how to live within their means, but the government seems not to know how!

11. America's fiscal problems threaten our security, our prosperity, and our survival.

12. By cutting 5 percent from spending per year and raising revenues by 5 percent per year, we could balance the budget in just five years.

13. We need heavy lifting on budget cuts and other priorities. Who will step up and make these decisions?

14. If any plan does not actually reduce government spending now, we need to avoid it like the plague!

15. Does Biden actually ask us to believe that his proposed spending would be funded with promises to pay for it in the deep future?

16. What is this liberal crap about killing Big Bird? Big Bird can survive without government subsidies!

17. "Government manipulated" can replace the term "seasonally adjusted."

18. Only a liberal could think spending can be cut by raising taxes.

15

Safe, Legal, and Frequent

We have the duty to protect the life of an unborn child.
—Ronald Reagan

1. Life is precious!

2. The abortion industry does not want this question even asked. "At what point in development do fetuses deserve societal protection?"

3. If a fetus is not alive at any point in its development, why is it necessary to kill it?

4. Only a liberal could name an abortion factory, Planned Parenthood!

5. If a fetus could communicate, what would it say to the notion of pro-choice?

6. Supporting unlimited and unrestrained abortion on demand does not make anyone pro-woman!

7. On January 22, 1973, the Roe v. Wade decision legalized abortion. And subsequently it has killed sixty-six million victims! Arguably the worst decision ever made by humans!

8. It is difficult to comprehend the gruesome impact of aborting over 55,000,000 unborn babies during the past forty-seven years!

9. Only a liberal could equate sucking live babies' brains out with women's healthcare!

10. Apparently, the words "born alive" are not descriptive enough to inform the liberal activists that babies, not fetuses, were killed!

11. Why is it so important to liberals that people don't have to pay for their own contraceptives?

12. What on earth is the defensible purpose of the government paying for the killing of babies?

13. If we took a poll of the preborn, we would find life is more popular, even for liberals!

14. Defining deviancy often begins with reframing the issue. Abortion and sexual promiscuity are now "defined" as "reproductive rights" of women!

15. Shouldn't we call Planned Parenthood something like Planned Nonparenthood?

16. Do democrats and the media really believe that all women are in favor of abortion on demand for any reason, at any time?

17. The oxymoronic liberal term for abortion is preventative healthcare!

18. The first choice of a liberal is to kill a preborn baby. If it can't be killed, the second choice is to make it dependent!

19. If the so-called pro-choice folks ever discovered they were wrong, how would they apologize?

20. Democrats and Planned Parenthood's commitment to abort any child, for any reason is unshakeable.

21. If we want to maintain each person's control of his or her own body, why not give babies the same courtesy?

22. Why isn't abortion on demand considered fetus torture? It's certainly more violent than waterboarding!

23. It's odd that environmentalists who see a link between earth and spotted owls cannot see the link between fetuses and babies!

24. Liberals don't want maternity leave—they want abortion leave!

25. What we call "women's reproductive rights" is really a woman's choice not to reproduce—after she's pregnant!

26. Democrats are not proponents of women when they promote abortion on demand!

27. Only liberals advocate for partial birth abortion—sucking babies' brains out born alive!

28. The baby-killing coat hangers are found in democratic baby-murdering factories, named Planned Parenthood!

29. It seems odd that so many democrats are demanding that other people pay for their birth control!

30. Apparently, the words "born alive" are not descriptive enough to inform the *New York Times* that babies, not fetuses, were killed!

31. Why do abortion advocates oppose holding abortion clinics to the same standards as hospital-style surgical centers?

32. Why isn't there more outrage over Kermit Barron Gosnell? The lack of Gosnell trial media coverage confirms that abortion is still liberalism's most sacred cow!

33. It's clear that the abortion industry does not want pregnant women to graphically sense just how alive their fetuses are!

34. The abortion industry has successfully (and sadly) marketed the killing of preborn babies as "women's rights" or "women's health!"

35. To the abortion industry, a heartbeat in a fetus means nothing!

36. The abortion industry touts "safe abortions." No abortion is "safe" for the baby!

37. One wonders how many women or mothers own abortion clinics!

38. Only a liberal believes trees have souls, but unborn babies are blobs of tissues!

39. If democrats really want fewer humans, they each have one life to give to their cause—their own!

16

Better than Steve Jobs

The chief business of the American people is business.
—Calvin Coolidge

You can't hate the job creators and love jobs.
—Arthur Laffer

1. For me, the lemonade stand is a symbol of free market capitalism. And capitalism is America's engine of prosperity.

2. If you are successful, sooner or later the left will come after you.

3. Profit promotes innovation!

4. Competition and innovation are the elements that generate improved products at lower prices. Without the profit motive, prosperity is impossible.

5. New businesses are the true engines of economic growth and job creation.

6. Business goes where it's appreciated and stays where it's well cared for.

7. Would you turn over control of your business to a career politician with no accomplishments?

8. Relieving regulatory pressure on business benefits everyone in the country.

9. Should a retail business increase revenues by raising prices (like the government raising taxes) or by opening new stores?

10. Every day we see the rules and regulations from DC bureaucrats who know nothing about running a business. Most could not even run a lemonade stand.

11. The democrats' rhetoric is probusiness but their actions are antibusiness creators. Is there any way this can make sense?

12. The reason business innovation begins in America is we don't have to be connected, of the right caste or race, or have government support for success!

13. The profit motive promotes innovation.

14. Liberals don't seem to understand that it's the profit motive that fosters innovation. And the profit motive disappears when it's taxed to death.

15. Competition and innovation are the elements that generate improved products at lower prices. Without the profit motive, neither will exist!

16. With few exceptions, the private sector needs to determine where to locate privately owned factories and personnel— not the government.

17. Free enterprise appears to be what the democrats refer to as the enemy!

18. The more we produce, the less we rely on others. Think about it.

19. Democrats think they can raise the middle class individuals while punishing those who would hire them.

20. How much different would any democrats be if they had ever run a small business where the buck did actually stop with them?

21. Is there anyone left who thinks Joe Biden could effectively manage a small business or even a lemonade stand?

22. Businesses go where they are appreciated and stay where they are well cared for. And they are not staying in liberal states.

17

All People, Created Somewhat Equal, under Government

As government expands, liberty contracts.
—Ronald Reagan

1. Limited government is not just a conservative slogan. It was born as an escape from tyranny and despotism. This must be taught!

2. Choose freedom, not bigger government! *Period*!

3. If it exists, big government liberals want to control it! *Period*!

4. If we want less political corruption, the only solution is less government!

5. Why don't we push for a bill that undoes all the exemptions and waivers (from laws we have to follow) that Congress has created for itself?

6. It is important to remember that government is seldom efficient or effective, irrespective of its noble intentions.

7. When will the American people vote for a government that isn't quite so greedy?

8. It's time to stop all the cushy little special favors our elected officials have granted themselves and their friends.

9. Are the hijinks of elected officials America's greatest risk, or is it the hidden power of career bureaucrats that should worry us?

10. If we eliminated the ability of Congress to give tax favors to constituents, would members still want the job?

11. Government needs to be limited not only by what it should do, but also by what it can actually do!

12. If you're just a hard-working, middle-class American, you *can't* afford the government's stupidity!

13. If we removed all the corrupt and dishonest politicians from Washington, how many would be left?

14. Baseline budgeting; off-budget, saved, or created job reports; phony unemployment rates; and debt/deficits numbers *all* are designed by the government to *deceive* the public!

15. The democrats have proven that government intrusiveness and overreach goes hand-in-hand with government dissembling and corruption!

16. What democrats miss is that in most cases, government is the problem not the solution!

17. It's time for Congress to do something meaningful, like get the wall money approved!

18. Now that Americans have seen the reality of big government (incompetence, waste, cronyism, politics)—smaller government sounds better!

19. One way to look at the national debt is that we have received twenty-two trillion dollars of government for which we have not yet paid!

20. Does anyone really assume all, or even most, of the existing government programs deliver what was promised?

21. The concept that the government should do only what the states and individuals cannot do better for themselves has been lost.

22. Government programs are measured against this question, "Would they do any good whatsoever even if they are not done well?"

23. We pay our government officials too much, their benefits are greater than ours, and they exempt themselves from the laws we follow!

24. It's time for us to rewrite all laws passed by Congress that allow for congressional exemptions!

25. Government for too long has thought of itself as superior to the citizenry!

26. If it weren't for self-dealing in Congress—there wouldn't be much dealing at all!

27. With their big buildings, fancy titles, legal exemptions, and short work weeks—Congress thinks it is royalty!

28. The congressional motto is "Good enough for thee—but not for me!"

29. Congressional help wanted: must be devious, corrupt, lazy, dissembling, and incompetent!

30. There is no reason for people to treat elected politicians like royalty!

31. There is no reason for we the people to allow elected politicians to treat themselves like royalty!

32. The rarest thing on earth might be politicians who deliver on their promises!

33. President Trump might be the rarest thing on earth—a politician who delivers on his promises!

34. Members of Congress take many actions many actions that are objectionable, but treating themselves like royalty takes the cake!

35. The real class divide in America is between the political class and everyone else.

36. The job of government is to protect our rights—not to hand out democratic bucks!

37. Legitimate government will protect freedom, preserve law and order, enforce private contracts, and foster competitive markets.

18

Fourth Branch of Government—Regulating Businesses Out of Business

Many people want the government to protect the consumer. A much more urgent problem is to protect the consumer from the government.
—Milton Friedman

1. Politicians love power—so most of their legislation and regulations are designed to increase it.

2. The one thing democrats and their regulators have successfully regulated is the growth in jobs!

3. The greatest danger to Americans is our fourth branch of government: unelected bureaucrats ruling us out of business!

4. Democrats are not afraid of pointless hyperregulation or job-killing policies!

5. Congress does not approve any new regulation. Regulations are strictly bureaucratic constructs!

6. Democrats are already defending this attempted regulatory overreach and have projected horrible consequences to delaying this regulation!

7. Liberalism means high taxes, suffocating regulations, frivolous lawsuits, unchecked illegal immigration, and rabid environmentalism!

8. What liberal politicians can't own, they want to control through excessive regulation and taxation!

9. Is there anything worse than unelected activists chasing their ideology with regulations?

10. Progressivism begins with excessive regulation of markets, property, and private enterprise but always end with government coercion!

11. A progressive commandment is "Thou shalt regulate businesses we don't like out of business!"

12. Progressives are primarily for big government and heavy-handed regulations. Both big government and big regulations favor large companies over small!

13. How many bureaucrats does the government employ to distort data? Answer—As many as it takes to turn reality into propaganda.

14. What is the hardest part about creating a new government bureaucracy? Finding a three-letter acronym that isn't already taken by the existing thousands of bureaucracies.

15. The more regulations the democrats impose on business, the more small businesses that cannot afford them suffer.

16. The democrats' anticapitalist regulations are their attempt to "fundamentally change" our economy—to the advantage of China and others.

17. Politicians do not write the laws they pass. Unelected, unionized, pensioned, civil-serviced protected bureaucrats *write*, *enact*, and *enforce* the laws of the Internal Revenue Service (IRS), the Environmental Protection Agency (EPA), and the Occupational Safety and Health Administration (OSHA).

18. The federal register grows every year. It never shrinks!

19. Liberals have successfully infiltrated the permanent bureaucracy and they show us their perverse power every day.

20. Liberal government is often about taking corruption and institutionalizing it!

19

Government Healthcare— Ever Been to the Veterans Affairs Medical Centers?

If you believe that health care is a public good to be guaranteed by the state, then a single-payer system is the next best alternative. Unfortunately, it is fiscally unsustainable without rationing.
—Charles Krauthammer

1. The whole point of Obamacare was to have it fail, so democrats could bring in single-payer government insurance!

2. Affordable care is just one of the things the Affordable Care Act (ACA) has failed to provide!

3. No matter what liberals say about Obamacare, it's still based on bribes, lies, coercions, and price controls.

4. The ACA doesn't make anything "affordable" and provides no additional "care;" it is just an "act!"

5. If you want to know what single-payer healthcare is like, ask veterans how long they wait for surgeries at a VA Medical Center.

6. If the government controls drugs and hospitals, it controls everything.

7. When liberals say Obamacare is "working," they mean the government is expanding and the bureaucracy is taking control.

8. The media is ignoring that Obamacare coverage eliminates most of the better doctors and hospitals!

9. The media refuses to acknowledge the obvious difference between health insurance and healthcare!

10. Somehow democrats managed to write the ACA—without reading it!

11. Obamacare is the law that liberals bribed through Congress!

12. We're from the government, and we're here to provide you healthcare—as we see fit!

13. Obamacare was presented as an act of charity for poor people, but it has turned out to be a tool for state power and government control!

14. One would think giving away "free" or highly subsidized healthcare coverage would have been easier!

15. Can you think of a more *ineffective* way to produce more doctors than paying them less and taxing them more?

16. Congressional members didn't read the ACA, but exempted themselves on instinct.

17. When we add the cost of state, federal, and employer healthcare bureaucracy costs to medical care, it just gets more expensive!

18. Trusting the government to "fix" Obamacare would be like trusting a plumber to do brain surgery.

19. If the government doesn't force roughly half the people to buy insurance at high prices, it can't afford to give the other half insurance for free!

20. If you like your plan, you can keep your plan is still a lie!

21. "You can keep your doctor" is still a lie!

20

Welfare and Disability—Moochers Are Needy Too!

We should measure welfare's success by how many people leave welfare, not by how many are added.
—Ronald Reagan

1. The conservative concept is simple. Help the truly needy and put the moochers back to work.

2. If welfare went to the truly poor and the truly needy, everyone would be for it.

3. Our welfare system is unsustainable, but worse than that, even though it can sound caring, it doesn't work!

4. The safety net is needed to treat the symptoms of poverty, but it does nothing to effect a cure!

5. One of the many feckless liberal attempts to address excessive dependency is to rename the assistance given. Don't call it welfare!

6. How many lives have been ruined by government dependency? Does government dependency do more harm than poverty?

7. Instead of calling our welfare programs a safety net, we might better call them a "safety trap."

8. Has the nation's safety net already been turned into a hammock?

9. Democrat doctrine is to pay people who don't work and tax people who do work!

10. Beyond progressives is the idea that the goal of welfare is to help people out of it, not into it!

11. Welfare government money should only go to these people: the poor and needy through no fault of their own, those who made bad choices, and those who earned it.

12. Do the people who sign the back of their paychecks really think they can do without the folks who sign the front?

13. For the democrats and their sycophant media friends, any cut in the projected growth in a welfare program is described as a "slash!"

14. Pathetically, it appears many of the unemployed have stopped claiming to be unemployed and now claim to be disabled!

15. How much will this apparently high level of disability fraud affect the truly disabled?

16. If we are to believe democrats, a democrat has already made millions of people "happy" by driving them out of the workforce!

17. Democrats do not count the long-term unemployed as unemployed. They count them as "people spending more family time!"

18. If higher government benefits encourage some not to work, do higher benefits also encourage some to stay in poverty?

19. Once we start government subsidies to people capable of supporting themselves, some will choose for the government to support them!

20. The government does not "give" any benefits. It first must confiscate from others to pay for that which it gives!

21. There are over 185 means-tested, government welfare programs, all run by permanent bureaucrats with no consequences to performing poorly! One trillion dollars is spent!

22. Have you ever known anyone who became successful based on a government job-training program? Me neither!

23. Is it possible that the democrats would rather see Americans unemployed and in need of government assistance?

21

Foreign Policy

Domestic policy can only defeat us; foreign policy can kill us.
—John F. Kennedy

1. A foreign policy of appeasement and wishful thinking only works in the faculty lounge!

2. Trump is putting America first by bolstering American influence by leading a coalition of strong nations by promoting security and prosperity around the world.

3. Maybe it's time for the US to quit trying to save Arabs and Muslims from other Arabs and Muslims and just take care of US interests!

4. The free trade agreements that Trump is now pushing are putting foreign nations on alert.

5. Russian Vladimir Putin might have been able to outthink Obama but not Trump. Trump has no flexibility.

6. When Israel pulled out of Gaza, it was to test a "two-state solution." Hamas turned Gaza into a huge military base!

7. Does anyone think democrats are pro-Israel or that democrats and Israeli Benjamin Netanyahu respect each other?

8. Is there anyone who still believes Iran is not attempting to build a nuclear weapon—except perhaps the United Nations (UN) and its inspectors?

9. With accelerating nuclear proliferation, the current notions of limited wars might soon come to an end! A sobering thought for all sides!

10. How is it that our enemies are expressing their "increased" hatred for Americans? These people already put bombs on their children to kill us!

11. When Obama sets a clear red line, the typical world response is, "What difference does it make?!"

12. Trump announced and recognized Jerusalem as the capital of Israel and ordered the relocation of the US embassy from Tel Aviv to Jerusalem.

13. Trump is refusing to allow the world's number one exporter of terror, Iran, to seize a nuclear bomb.

14. Trump refuses to allow Communist China to exploit US trade deficits for its benefit.

15. Is it time for the United States to quit going to war, if the issues are not significant enough for us to go all out to win?

16. If we are not prepared to fight to win using all of our military tools and tactics, perhaps we need to stay at the negotiating table and not the battlefield.

17. If we do not have the will to win a particular war, collateral damages included, then we need to stay out or quit the war.

18. Our attempt to fight surgical, limited engagement, politically sensitive wars is what has kept us in Afghanistan so long!

19. Wars are to be avoided. But if a war must be fought, we must fight it to win with everything we have! The word conquer comes to mind!

20. War is not foggy—it is brutal and unforgiving. If we must go to war, we owe it to our troops to use all of our might to win every battle!

21. War is hell. When we try to make it less than hell through politics, we get too many of our troops killed or maimed.

22. The US has developed this political notion that we can wage a war where only the bad guys get killed and the "innocents" can be spared.

23. Where in history has limited engagement war worked? When in history has the fog of war cleared so that only the bad die?

24. It sickens me to see our leaders follow a strategy of "limited war" in order to preserve political capital.

25. If the US is not willing to win and win big, perhaps fighting needs to be avoided. If fighting cannot be avoided—*win*!

26. Maybe it is time for the US to quit trying to save Arabs and Muslims from other Arabs and Muslims—and just take care of US interests!

27. Americans first. America first!

22

United Nations— Unelected Nitwits

The United Nations was set up not to get us to heaven, but only to save us from hell.
—Winston Churchill

1. Everyone, except the democrats, knows the United Nations (UN) is a feckless anticapitalist, anti-American organization of leftist bureaucrats!

2. A democrat slogan is, "We support the UN because we like spending the money and the lunches are terrific!"

3. The Democratic National Convention supports the UN— because it's the only organization that is less effective and more corrupt than it is!

4. If the UN halted its regular trumped-up denunciations of Israel, what would be its new purpose?

5. The UN says that humans are "extremely likely" the main cause of global warming. These liberal geniuses each have one life to give to their cause!

6. Who cannot see that the UN is promoting the notion of global warming to get its hands on other people's money?

7. The UN is where meaningful and effective action goes to die!

8. The UN is neither united nor competent to take on tough assignments. Mission failure is a typical UN outcome.

9. If the US funds the UN at all, perhaps voting rights need to be proportionate to funding contributions!

10. Apparently, when we send a bunch of international politicians to solve a junk science problem, we get UN carbon credits!

11. One thing the UN is not is united!

12. How many times are the words "feckless, spineless, weak, worthless, and feeble" used in the UN charter?!

13. The UN actually has peacekeeping operations. Why are they there and what do they do?!

14. In an unrelated event, the UN asked its representatives to reduce the number of countries where it rapes and pillages!

15. Has the US given more to the UN than it has to deserving Americans?

16. With countries like China and Iran on the UN human rights council, why does the US support this antiwomen, anti-Christian, anti-Israel, and prodictator organization?

23

Budget—Numbers Are What We Say They Are

Balanced budget requirements seem more likely to produce accounting ingenuity than genuinely balanced budgets.
—Thomas Sowell

1. The so-called budget compromise that democrats want is a compromise that keeps overspending and overtaxing!

2. Imagine a picture of democrats not at work, not approving a budget. It's easier than you think, isn't it?!

3. Who would have thought our political representatives would have such difficulty living within our means!

4. The budget fight will continue because republicans want us to live within our means, and democrats want to keep buying votes at whatever it takes!

5. Democrats want to spend money on ill-conceived and ill-run government programs!

6. Every elected federal politician knows that our budget problems are primarily entitlement related and each one has known this for years!

7. How is it we elected such fools and knaves to represent us? We continue to see their "blame the other guy" priority!

8. If excessive pay and pensions for government employees at all levels is not addressed, there is no hope to balance the budget—ever!

9. If government accounting trickery becomes a crime, the entire government could be at risk of prosecution!

10. If a private company cooked the books like the government—the owners would be locked up in jail! Rightfully so!

11. Many economists correctly point out that it's more important to shrink government than to balance the budget via taxes or borrowing!

12. The fight for a fiscal budget needs to begin with a legal limit on revenues (taxes)—not more than 20 percent of the gross domestic product (GDP).

13. If we legally limit the level of government revenues, perhaps we can then begin to set national priorities.

14. How surprising was it that the vaunted Congressional Budget Office was so easily misled by democrats? Answer— Not at all!

15. Any democrat budget proposal for spending cuts means to make lives shorter, harder, and unhealthier. Democrat demagoguery already started!

16. Congress is doing more budget dithering! Can you say term limits!

17. A democratic slogan is "Tax, spend, borrow, blame, and pander!"

24

Economy

Government's view of the economy . . . If it moves, tax it. If it keeps moving, regulate it. And if it stops moving, subsidize it.
—Ronald Reagan

1. It's the economy, stupid.

2. If we line up all the economists in the world and ask what is coming, all we get is a long line of economists!

3. Why don't the democrats address our exceptional economy? One answer is that they do not know how!

4. When the economy is foundering, politicians first deny, then rationalize and blame, then change the subject!

5. It's more important to shrink the government than to balance the budget via taxes or borrowing!

6. Keynesian economics assumes moving money from your left pocket to your right pocket can make you richer!

7. The reason we are finally seeing some positive numbers in the economy is that it took entrepreneurs and Trump to overcome Obama's policies!

8. The only "weakness" shown in the American economy has been exacerbated by the weakness shown in the Democratic Party!

9. Don't spend more than you make.

10. Don't borrow more than you can repay.

11. Don't print so much new money that the currency is devalued.

12. Don't tax achievers so much that they lose the incentive to achieve.

13. Plan and save for a rainy day.

14. Democrats define economic justice as not having to bear the consequences of their previous bad decisions.

15. Even if the economy starts to grow or shrink (which is unlikely) due to the uncertainty of COVID-19, Americans will still choose personal responsibility over collectivism!

16. Of course, when economists use the term "smooth the data," they mean "cheat" or "fudge" or "misrepresent."

17. Biden might know we need to promote economic innovation, but he is trapped by a base that wants more regulations that impede growth!

18. Americans want job growth and economic expansion more than they want redistribution and a hostile environment for business.

19. Americans know that private sector businesses create enduring jobs. They will see through Biden's demonizing of job creators!

20. When it comes to American economics, Biden is like a man dying of thirst giving grief to the only people with water!

25

Fiscal Cliff

Government is the great fiction, through which everybody
endeavors to live at the expense of everybody else.
—**Claude-Frédéric Bastiat**

1. The proper name for the fiscal cliff is the Democratic Party's agenda.

2. Take us over the cliff. It's time to quit playing this dangerous game!

3. So the democrats demand tax hikes now with a promise of spending cuts later—again.

4. Democrats demand a one to two trillion dollar tax boost and an unlimited credit card. It's the liberal mindset!

5. The so-called fiscal cliff (rising taxes and spending cuts) might be a factor, but democrat's anti-prosperity policies loom large!

6. The predominant belief in Washington, DC, is that the government will not fix the fiscal cliff problem but will kick it down the road—again!

7. Are you kidding me? Inaction is the democrats' default position!

8. The sad part about this fiscal cliff matter is that everyone in Washington, DC, knows the solution, but can't get past their own political theaters!

9. Taxes will go up, regulations will increase, the military will be cut, budget cuts will be put off and spending will rise. Democrats will be celebrating!

10. Democrats do not care about US economic problems. They want to punish the successful, grow government, and post a political win!

11. What Congress is calling a fiscal cliff deal does not even begin to address our economic issues!

12. Too many Americans are addicted to "free stuff" from the government, and there is not enough money to pay for all of it!

13. The fiscal cliff issues will, if not addressed, affect matters short-term, but democrats' anti-prosperity policies will last and last!

14. The US fiscal prescription is to limit government revenues to 20 percent GDP, measure the efficacy of each government program, and let the people decide priorities! Limit government!

15. Of course, my fiscal prescription would require common sense, business acumen, and constitutional amendments. The first two are scarce in government, and the latter is time-consuming and difficult. But that is my solution!

16. If politicians really don't like raising the debt ceiling, perhaps they need to follow the first rule of fiscal responsibility: make more than you spend!

26

Internal Revenue Service

A government that robs Peter to pay Paul can
always depend on the support of Paul.
—George Bernard Shaw

1. IRS abuse—the definition of oxymoronic!

2. Democrats have officially named and declared April 15 a
    national holiday—Redistribution Day!

3. When did Cincinnati become a sanctuary for "rogue" IRS
    agents committing unethical and criminal activities?

4. Is there anything more telling about the inefficiency,
    ineffectiveness, and corruption of government than the IRS
    investigation?

5. The IRS is a nonpartisan, objective government agency, just
    like ABC, CNN, MSNBC, NBC, or CBS are nonpartisan
    objective news organizations!

6. Is it possible the IRS employees are incompetent at their jobs, political in their targeting, but capable of getting away with rank deception?

7. Why is it that so many democrats defend and support the IRS? Do they really want that on their résumés?

8. If democrats could just sic the IRS or the Occupational Safety and Health Administration (OSHA) or the Department of Justice (DOJ) on the border, perhaps we could make progress!

9. Do we even know how many IRS employees are not political or corrupt? No one was fired!

10. Is there anyone who believes former IRS director Lois Lerner's emails were "accidentally" lost?

11. Isn't it notable that not even one democrat can see the potential for any corruption in the IRS targeting scandal!

12. Will liberals and the media still be fine with the IRS targeting political groups, when it's their groups being targeted? Not!

13. Let's not forget that the IRS rewarded itself with big bonuses *after* the scandal.

14. The problem is that the government has expanded itself well beyond the authority it was originally given!

15. As long as it's conservative groups getting the runaround from the IRS, democrats will not see a smidgen of corruption!

16. The IRS targeted conservative groups for tax audits. No one was fired. They are still at work. Period.

17. Democrats and Obama still insist that the IRS targeting of his political opponents was just "confusion and coincidence." Really?

18. With IRSGate, ObamaGate, TrumpGate, WitchHuntGate, RussiaGate, SpyGate, BenghaziGate, AP PhoneRecordsGate— the DNC is now considered a gated community! Throw away the keys!

19. Is there any chance that the IRS targeting scandal was entirely the doing of IRS manager Lois Lerner? No!

20. Did IRS Director of the Exempt Organizations Unit Lois Lerner really say, "I'm not good at math"? It appears she did!

21. Just exactly how much evidence has "disappeared" in the IRS targeting investigation?

22. Everyone knows the current federal tax code is riddled with corruption, is too complex, and is filled with indefensible loopholes, but Congress will not act!

23. For Congress, the federal tax code represents a major source of its power over the rest of us. Congress will not give up this power without a fight!

24. If the tax code were reduced from 80,000 pages of hidden favors to 20 pages of flat or fair tax, no tax experts would be needed.

25. Let's eliminate all corporate and other subsidies with some form of flat tax with no deductions—hidden or otherwise.

26. Our current tax code has 80,000 pages of hidden favors for corporate and many other constituencies. Take tax breaks away from politicians!

27. Simplifying the tax code can be done in fewer than twenty pages, but Congress is reluctant to give up so much of its power over us.

28. Everyone knows the 80,000-page federal tax code is filled with special deals for favored industries, but few in Congress will address it!

29. The federal tax code and certain state tax codes give power to politicians, so it is unlikely that the feds or the states will materially simplify the codes!

30. The solution is simple. Tax everything once when it is sold and eliminate the IRS completely. Of course, the income tax would need to be outlawed.

31. Chief Justice John Marshall's most famous quote is this: "The power to tax is the power to destroy."

32. Why do we have 80,000 pages of loopholes and hidden favors in our tax code? It's the tool that Congress uses to fund its campaigns!

33. Does anyone know how many special tax breaks for members of Congress are hidden in the tax code? I wish I knew!

34. The primary objective of democrats (taxing millionaires) might bring down some of the rich, but it won't serve to raise up the middle class!

35. Taxing millionaires is not an egalitarian economic plan; it is just an attempt to satisfy vengeful envy and blame others for our woes!

36. A huge flaw in the democrats' tactic of raising taxes is the assumption that any new money given to the government would be well spent. It won't!

37. One of the primary flaws in the liberal argument for higher taxes is the implied assumption that any new government money will be spent well!

38. Liberals ignore the fact that new government revenue from higher taxes will not only be spent poorly, it will be spent on the wrong things!

39. If we give new money to liberal politicians, they will not fix our schools. They will give money to the education bureaucracy and to public sector unions!

40. If we do not give new money to liberal politicians to buy votes, they are threatening to gut national defense. This tells us much!

41. If the left was really concerned about unequal political clout by the rich, it would begin by supporting some form of flat tax!

42. It is the 80,000-page tax code that hides many of the political favors and biases gained by lobbying! Throw it out—go flat!

43. Since 1919, lobbyists, politicians, and their friends have been carving out special deductions, loopholes, and deductions from the tax code to the tune of 80,000-plus pages.

44. The solution is a flat or fair tax! Abolish the IRS. Everyone pays 20 percent! Equality!

27

Taxes

*I am in favor of cutting taxes under any circumstances and
for any excuse, for any reason, whenever it's possible.*
—Milton Friedman

1. Only a liberal could think spending can be cut by raising taxes!

2. Only in America could rich people—who pay 86 percent of all income taxes—be accused of not paying their "fair share" by people who don't pay any at all!

3. If we give the government more money under any pretense, it will waste it, use it to buy votes, and expand its own power!

4. Rich is a term of art used by liberals to rationalize the taking of private property fairly earned by hard-working Americans!

5. Do you ever get the feeling that no matter how much the rich paid in taxes, it would not be enough for the democrats?

6. Is there a tax of any nature that liberals do not support?

7. Everyone, except our elected politicians and employed bureaucrats, knows it's time to simplify the tax code and eliminate the IRS!

8. Increased taxes means taking money from job creators, filtering it through the government, and then giving some back to non-job creators!

9. Whatever you tax, you get less of.

10. When you tax, things get more expensive. When things get more expensive, fewer people buy them. It's really that simple.

11. All taxes do is transfer money from the private sector (individuals) to the public sector (government).

12. Liberals support higher taxes to milk the successful and make the less successful more dependent on government largess!

13. If a conservative is left with any money whatsoever after taxes and government fees, liberals consider that unfair!

14. When you don't believe in the concept of personal responsibility, it's easy to tax more and give all the credit for success to government!

15. Why would anyone want to give an ineffective, inefficient, and corrupt organization like the US government more of his or her money?

16. If more people had to pay taxes, they would be for smaller government.

17. There is no incentive to spend wisely when you are spending money that is not your own on other people.

18. Liberals tax cigarettes and alcohol to reduce consumption. So, why do they tax capital and job creators?

19. Have you heard even one democrat attempt to defend that 40 percent of Americans pay no federal income tax and get a *refund*? Me neither!

20. Have you heard even one democrat attempt to defend that 47 percent of Americans pay no federal income tax? Me neither!

21. The bottom 40 percent of earners were actually paid cash by the IRS. April 15 has a different meaning to them!

22. Did Biden really say that taxing the rich (for example) is the kind of proposal supported by both democrats and republicans? He must have missed the debate on this one!

23. Elimination of the capital gains tax would immediately draw needed capital investment into America from around the world!

24. To a conservative, tax reform means ending special interest tax breaks and lowering the overall tax rate!

25. When companies pay lower taxes, fewer taxes get passed on to the general public.

26. What would happen to American politics if the media and the people actually held politicians responsible for their mistakes?

27. Because the top 10 percent of earners pay 70 percent of all federal income taxes, what is your definition of fair share?

28. Democratic motto: We will tax you in the morning. We will tax you late at night. We will tax you when it's dark out. We will tax you when it's bright!

29. Raising taxes puts *more* money in the hands of politicians. Think about it!

30. Each year, democrats will want more tax hikes to address their continuing spending problems.

31. There is no way that transferring money from the private sector to the public sector creates prosperity for anyone except elected officials.

32. What low taxes do is keep more money in the productive hands of entrepreneurs and away from unproductive government spending!

33. Our problem in the US is spending, not taxing. The whole concept of living within our means has been lost in Congress!

34. If all people are created equal and all people are treated equally under the law, why do some people pay taxes while others do not?!

35. Are the "Trump tax cuts" soon to be known as the "democrats' tax increases"?

36. A primary flaw in the liberal mindset is that a generous welfare state can be sustained only with other people's money!

37. Democrats don't think it is "fair" that half the nation who doesn't pay income taxes doesn't get more help from the half who does!

38. There is no history showing that more taxes given to the government will lead to deficit reduction. History shows more taxes lead to more spending!

39. History shows that more taxes lead to bigger government, not reduced deficits. I think almost every democrat knows this!

40. Make America competitive and create jobs—lower corporate tax rates!

28

Housing Banking

*Riskier mortgage lending practices, imposed by government, were
what set the stage . . . for the financial disasters that followed.*
—Thomas Sowell

1. Isn't giving loans to people unable to pay them what caused
   the housing bust and initiated the financial crisis?

2. It was the housing crisis, caused largely by subprime lending
   to unqualified buyers, that began the recession!

3. Many are against any type of bailout, but others think banks
   are the exception because the financial system is such a
   lynchpin in the economy.

4. We keep hearing "move forward or return to the failed
   policies of the past." The failed policies began with Fannie
   Mae and Freddie Mac mortgages.

5. When the government began incentivizing or coercing lenders to make loans to underqualified borrowers, the housing bubble began.

6. When those underqualified borrowers failed to make their house payments, the housing bubble burst!

7. There is blame to go around, but the housing bust began with liberal lending policies promoted by democrats!

8. Although Bush did not do enough to stop these politicized lending standards, it was democrats who promoted and protected them.

9. The republicans need to rebut the implication that the recession was caused by Bush deregulation policies and do it now!

10. If we allow these false democratic talking points to go unchallenged, people will start to believe them.

11. Just because the housing bust (which triggered the recession) occurred on Bush's watch, that doesn't mean Bush was responsible!

12. Bush was not guilt free regarding the housing bust. He could have done more to thwart bad lending policies, but he did not start them!

13. When democrats say, "Let's not return to the failed Bush policies that got us into this mess," republicans need to correct the history and talk about the Dodd-Frank Act!

14. When democrats say, "Let's not return to the failed Bush policies that got us into this mess," republicans need to remind everyone that Obama was Bush on steroids!

15. The government is doing its best to keep the housing industry from completing its normal recovery cycle!

16. Housing prices need to fall to levels where buying existing houses becomes attractive to potential purchasers. Democrats' programs hinder!

17. In other words, it was democratic lending policies (not Bush policies) that were the source of most of our current economic distress!

29

Federal Reserve

The Federal Reserve answers to no one.
—Ronald Reagan

1. As the Federal Reserve System (Fed) continues to control nearly every financial market, we once again find that central planning does not work!

2. The longer the Fed keeps printing money (buying securities), the more it helps big banks and hurts small savers!

3. It's time to eliminate the Fed dual mandate (full employment and control inflation). The purpose of the Fed needs to be limited.

4. The purpose of the Fed needs to be limited to controlling inflation (protecting the buying power of the US dollar).

5.   The Fed prefers to look at "core" inflation (inflation without food and energy). I wish that worked for my family, but we eat and use energy!

6.   My guess is the Fed will keep experimenting with the money supply as long as it still is driven by its current dual mandate!

7.   It matters not whether the Fed dual mandate began in 1977 or was based on legislation in 1946. It is wrong.

8.   The Fed mandate needs to be limited to protecting the buying power of the dollar (inflation) because it does not have the tools to do more!

9.   When the Fed attempts to create full employment, it runs the risk of allowing the dollar to inflate and lose its buying power!

10.   The problem the Fed has is a symptom of all government— the natural tendency is to grow. Every department of the government is always trying to get bigger.

11.   The primary problem with this "government wants to get bigger" tendency—is that it often succeeds!

12.   The Fed cannot solve our financial or housing crisis because our current economic issues are fiscal not monetary!

13.   The fix to current economic woes is to reform the tax code (lower flat or fair tax with no deductions), reform entitlements, and encourage success!

14. The Fed dual mandate is what keeps it meddling in the market. We need stability, not intervention!

15. Policies from Congress, not more short-term stimulus from the Fed, are necessary for restoring growth.

16. What we have now is, in effect, the printing of money without a corresponding increase in production or productivity!

17. The Fed likely sustained its stimulus program, because it knew Obama's economy would continue to suck!

18. The Fed is charged by Congress to accomplish full employment and stable prices. This is the same Congress whose members cannot even pay their own parking tickets.

19. For economists, they guess and the Fed targets 2 percent inflation as a compromise—with no consequence for being wrong.

30

Public Unions

The process of collective bargaining . . .
cannot be transplanted into the public service.
—**Franklin D. Roosevelt**

1. Do unions bargain more for workers or more for politicians?

2. The unionization of federal workers became the foundation of the permanent bureaucracy as the fourth branch of government!

3. Government workers demand that the people pay them for the rest of their lives.

4. It's well past time to throw out public sector unions and to overhaul civil service regulations!

5. Public unions work for the unions and steal from the middle class to feather union workers' comfortable nests!

6. The unholy alliance between elected politicians and public unions is now bearing its ugly fruit, which is both pervasive and toxic!

7. The real class warfare is not rich versus poor, it is the unelected unionized government bureaucrats and politicians versus the taxpayers!

8. Doesn't it appear that while Congress was taking "special care" of public employee pensions that it also took "special care" of its own?

9. Is government the problem or the solution? Unions argue the need for more government (more unionized workers), then they argue they need more protection as government grows!

10. A choice to keep public union collective bargaining is a choice to keep political corruption!

11. Who wants to pay for expanded public retirement and healthcare entitlements?

12. Collective bargaining by public unions needs to go the way of the dinosaurs.

13. How long has it been since unions had any material agenda other than increasing their own dues and buying influence in Congress?

14. A public union has but one objective: raid the public treasury!

15. It's not union busting or bashing, it's just fiscal responsibility, returning constitutional rights to taxpayers and corruption bashing!

16. The dispute is not about public employees. It is about the unholy relationship among union leaders, money, and politicians

17. The government did not bail out General Motors shareholders or bondholders or nonunion employees. The United Auto Workers (UAW) union was the big winner!

18. There is much logic to General Motors being called "Government Motors" but more logic to calling it "UAW Motors!"

19. Why do we allow public union workers to be paid more for the same job than what a private sector job pays?

20. The real class warfare is not rich versus poor—it is the entrenched political class and public unions versus the taxpayers!

31

Energy

Energy is essential to meeting our basic needs.
—World Health Organization

1. Abolishing the Department of Energy is nut-cutting energy. It does not produce any energy!

2. Why is it that so many Americans go along with the Democratic Party anti-energy policies that seek to destroy the American way of life?

3. Even though the left, the media, and the government know we use less and have more energy, liberals still will not drill! Trump drills.

4. Okay, so explain why liberals continue to fight oil exports and limit oil refineries!

5. Could it be that electric cars are actually greater polluters when we take into account electricity usage, manufacturing emissions, and toxic disposal?

6. For democrats, when oil or gasoline prices go up, it's the speculators. When oil or gasoline prices go down, it's the democrats!

7. The left refuses to drill for oil.

8. Is the democrats' war against coal an environmental thing, an ideological thing, or just a "gets more votes than it loses" thing?

9. Every subsidy to one citizen who installs solar panels must be paid by another who does not!

10. Democrats still refuse to finish the Keystone Pipeline System.

11. Politically correct energy speech will not keep us in affordable or abundant energy! But instead of drilling, that's the plan!

12. Liberals still push "green energy" even though gigantic windmills kill birds and solar panels create toxic waste.

13. A democratic slogan is "Our energy policy is like our Department of Energy—neither produces any energy!"

14. Biden and the democrats will stop at nothing to shut down coal plants.

15. Why do the democrats want all of us to freeze to death with no energy?

16. Democrat policies have been designed to drive up the cost of energy in the name of reducing pollution!

17. How many "protected" birds must die from windmill blades before environmentalists notice?

18. How much subsidy per bird do the democrats pay for solar power plants to incinerate our flying friends?

19. Nuclear power is clean and efficient energy.

32

Environmental Protection Agency

*Preservation of our environment is not a liberal or
conservative challenge, it's common sense.*
—Ronald Reagan

1. We already have Congress to make laws; we don't need the
    Environmental Protection Agency (EPA).

2. The Endangered Species Act, the Clean Water Act, and
    the Clean Air Act turned out to be twisted engines of
    antigrowth extremism.

3. Why is it the priority of environmentalists to instigate
    conflict against private property owners and not to reduce/
    prevent pollution?

4. The greatest danger to Americans is our fourth branch of government: unelected bureaucrats ruling us out of business!

5. Is the EPA ever for anything that doesn't restrict economic growth?

6. There are always too many fools who believe that giving bureaucrats more authority and money will bring a solution!

7. It's time to stop the bureaucratic rulemaking to bypass Congress and the American people!

8. The EPA admits that its Clean Power Plan is not about pollution control!

9. The best "jobs plan" that Biden could offer would be to close the EPA, the National Labor Relations Board (NLRB), and the Department of Energy. And then just stay out of the private sector completely!

10. The EPA is meeting democrats' promise to make coal plants unprofitable and therefore unfeasible.

11. Government central planners, whether we call them czars or EPA bureaucrats, have a long history of failure.

12. Nearly everyone is for reducing and eliminating pollution—but not by putting viable and needed industries out of business.

13. No doubt once the world found fire, environmentalists began protesting.

14. If you believe the government, there was no, or very little, severe weather before people started burning fossil fuels.

15. Who exactly thinks the delta smelt bait fish is worth more than human life or productive farming?

16. What bothers anti-fracking zealots most is that it makes money, creates jobs, and increases energy independence!

17. With the Clean Air Act, do democrats want to reduce pollution or American prosperity?

18. What environmentalists want is to stop all human development! It's just that simple. They want fewer people, fewer houses, and fewer businesses!

19. State and federal environmental studies and the Endangered Species Act are key tools that liberals use to stop development!

20. Abuse of these laws and regulations is all too common when liberals want to control our lives in the name of environmentalism!

33

The Great Big Snowball

Communism doesn't work because people like to own stuff.
—Frank Zappa

1. If we fail to teach our children the essential truths of government, politics, and liberalism's historic failures—they will learn them the hard way!

2. What is the difference between a democRAT, a socialist, a communist, a liberal, and a progressive? Answer—The spelling!

3. When did educated people begin to believe a company will practically build itself, once the government provides the roads?

4. The primary problem with big government socialism is sooner or later when you live beyond your means, you run out of means!

5. Liberals lust for redistribution of income, as long as it's not their income being redistributed!

6. Confiscation, coercion, and control are the heart and soul of liberalism and socialism.

7. The inexorable problem with the notion of a socialist utopia is that it does not and cannot exist!

8. In the vernacular of democrats, the concept of "fair share" still means "You work—I spend!"

9. Socialism is an idea so great, it has to be mandatory.

10. Socialism equals shared misery for the masses and special privileges for the politically connected.

11. Pandering is what liberals do to buy votes. Vote for liberals and they will give you other people's stuff!

12. Why is it so many liberals seek to impose their notion of an acceptable lifestyle on the rest of us?

13. Do democrats really think the US would be better off if we were all poor, as long as we were "equal"?

14. If liberals are so compassionate, why do so many embrace the entrenched poverty and oppression of Cuba and Venezuela?

15. Socialism is the tyranny to believe in the power of state rights over individual rights!

16. US ghettos are driven by liberal ideology, forged by unions, and bankrupted by self-serving democrats catering to parasites!

17. Liberals lust for redistribution of income, as long as it's not their income being redistributed!

18. The problem with central planning, even when it's altruistic and not politically motivated for personal gain, is that it doesn't work!

19. Liberals require coercion, while conservatives rely on the marketplace!

20. Only a liberal would trade the unequal blessings of capitalism for the equal misery of socialism.

34

Property Rights

You own your own labor, you earn it, you own it.
It is your right—your life, your property.
—Ayn Rand

1. Property rights means what is yours is yours. They can't take it from you.

2. One's rights to capital, land, and the fruits of one's labor are being redistributed to the government.

3. Government continues to whittle away property rights.

4. Ultimately, behind attacks on property rights is the notion that the government owns all income, which it does not.

5. Behind attacks on property rights is the notion that the government leaves us only what it doesn't demand.

6. In America, it is the government that works for the people and not the other way around.

7. The Kelo v. City of New London decision allowed local governments to take the property of some individuals for the benefit of others. The Supreme Court gutted the "public use" restriction on eminent domain—democrat redistribution of property.

8. Property rights cannot and do *not* exist in socialist states. This is kept hidden by the American left.

9. A conservative believes in respect for individual property rights.

10. Property rights help create an atmosphere that allows people the chance for personal and business success.

11. Property rights means we own what we have earned and no one can take it away from us.

12. The US Constitution provides explicitly for the protection of private property in the Fifth and Fourteenth Amendments.

13. The Fifth Amendment states: *"Nor be deprived of life, liberty, or property, without due process of law; nor shall private property be taken for public use, without just compensation."*

14. The Fourteenth Amendment states: *"No State shall make or enforce any law which shall abridge the privileges or immunities of citizens of the United States; nor shall any State deprive any person of life, liberty, or property, without due process of law."*

15. Margaret Thatcher said, "There can be no liberty unless there is economic liberty."

16. Property rights ensure that a person owns what he has earned and that what is owned remains owned until one decides to sell it.

35

Wages and Inequality

A society that puts equality before freedom will get neither.
—Milton Friedman

1. Where did democrats learn to live within someone else's means? Answer—Everywhere they went!

2. Some people hate capitalism but expect a capitalist to provide them a high-paying job with great benefits.

3. In a "perfect" liberal world, the maker of inferior products is paid the same as the maker of superior products!

4. If America raises the minimum wage to fifteen dollars an hour, then perhaps it ought to lower welfare to the same amount!

5. There would not be so much wage inequality if liberals didn't hold so many people down!

6. Minimum wage is a liberal's way of deferring the need for education and training by subsidizing incompetence!

7. Once again, liberals want to ensure equality of outcome by bringing down the top instead of raising up the bottom.

8. Before America needs a minimum wage hike, it needs jobs. Higher wages but fewer jobs is not a solution!

9. We don't need a minimum wage law that creates unemployment; we need a maximum wage law for government workers!

10. Too many liberals think calling communism "income inequality" makes it better!

11. Disparaging earned success in the name of equality is a defining element/tactic of Marxism!

12. A democrat knows the minimum wage is intended to be a gateway job for new and unskilled workers. It was a wage never intended to support a family!

13. Apparently, the way liberals want to deal with what they call "income inequality" is to do away with high-paying jobs!

14. Income equality means that politicians should be paid fifteen dollars an hour, tops! They should make the same as the burger place employees who do more work!

15. Liberals seem willing to trade a massive increase in teenage and low-skilled unemployment for a higher minimum wage for a few!

16. The liberal mandate of equality of outcomes for all requires a loss of liberty and property for many!

17. Inequality equals injustice except when it comes to liberal power and control!

18. Because the top 10 percent of earners pay 70 percent of all federal income taxes, what is your definition of "fair share"?

19. If it isn't a living wage, why would you work there?

20. Where do politicians get the numbers to decide minimum wage?

21. Minimum wage isn't meant to support a family of four.

22. The only way to ensure income equality is to keep everyone poor. Cuba's been trying it for over forty years!

23. Competition for individual success (unequal outcomes) is the driver that creates societal benefits!

24. Attempts to equalize outcomes for the collective necessarily include diminished liberties for individuals!

25. The "social justice" of paying union wages based on seniority necessarily overpays poor workers and underpays top performers!

26. History is clear that higher minimum wage laws generate high unemployment in teens and low skilled workers. Sounds good—does harm!

27. Trump fixes things and creates wealth. Democrats regulate things and redistribute wealth!

28. Why do liberals want to bring women down to be equal to men? Liberal logic!

29. Has it occurred to liberals that the possibility of "income inequality" is a primary reason people immigrate to the United States?

30. The more we produce, the less we rely on others. Think about it.

31. Income inequality is inevitable because there are so many factors. Income equality is communism.

32. Let's just ban all corporate profits and high wages. Then we'll be done with this debate!

33. Except for the truly disabled and victims of tragedy, talent, innovation, and hard work are the true remedies for income inequality.

34. Less than 1 percent of Americans are paid minimum wage. Perhaps letting employers compete for workers isn't so bad?

35. Skilled labor unions support minimum wage because it makes unskilled workers uncompetitive.

36. If democrats cared about unskilled laborers, they would work to abolish minimum wage laws.

37. Employers, especially small business owners, have limited budgets for employees. Higher minimum wage means fewer jobs, period.

38. There are almost no jobs that Americans will not do. There are only wage rates that Americans will not accept!

39. Minimum wage laws do not create any jobs—zero jobs.

36

Political Correctness

Political correctness is tyranny with manners.
—Charlton Heston

1. One word best describes political correctness—censorship!

2. Political correctness is a left-wing invention designed to create "victims!"

3. Brainless political correctness and hysterical overreaction are at the center of the liberal thought police!

4. Political correctness begins with identity politics and ends with an infringement on free speech!

5. Political correctness is an authoritarian endeavor to police speech in the name of protecting hurt feelings!

6. Political correctness is dangerous because it hides the truth.

7. Political correctness is how we got the term "undocumented worker." Are criminal killers soon to be "justice-involved individuals"?

8. The American left has succumbed to appeasement and political correctness, in all it does or doesn't do!

9. For too many people the concepts of right and wrong have been replaced by the term "legal!"

10. Have you heard about the left's demand for "trigger warnings" to alert students that uncomfortable content might be coming?

11. If you think no one should ever have to see or hear anything discordant or challenging, don't go outside.

12. A nation of sheep breeds a government of wolves.

37

Liberalism— Progressively Worse

The trouble with Socialism is that eventually
you run out of other people's money.
—Margaret Thatcher

1. Liberals believe the present is a time for them, while conservatives believe the present is a time for making society better for their children!

2. Accusing others of what you are actually doing was a favorite tactic of Lenin! Democrats have used it "religiously" since 1829!

3. The only difference between parasites and liberals is that parasites understand that killing their host wouldn't be good for them.

4. The worst part of capitalism for many liberals is that in this system, success often requires work!

5. For a democrat, "I take full responsibility, that's on me" translates to "You can't touch me for this!"

6. The reason democrats try so hard to get reelected is that they would hate to have to make a living under the laws they've passed.

7. What does a liberal call someone who breaks the law? Answer—A constituent!

8. Liberals are okay with the concept of work, as long as someone else is doing it!

9. The liberal rap against capitalism is that it doesn't allow everyone to win! The conservative rap against big government is that it allows only the government to win!

10. Liberals require a dumbed-down permanent welfare underclass to stay in power!

11. Apparently liberals require a bit more study. How does getting rich by selling innovative products hurt the poor?

12. Social justice is a term made up by liberals to justify their taking of property from political opponents to give to their favorite donors!

13. Liberals appear undaunted, despite their repeated demonstrations of cluelessness!

14. The liberal promise is for a socialist paradise paid for with other people's money, an age-old scam fraught with deception!

15. Have you noticed how many liberals display extreme incivility while they are demanding more civility?

16. If you are feeling optimistic about your economics, you're either a one-percenter or about to receive your welfare check!

17. Don't worry! The democrats won't destroy our liberties—they will display them next to the US Constitution under glass at the Smithsonian!

18. For liberals, logic is not an issue, facts are not a concern, and the truth is optional!

19. Liberals avoid facts so they can stay with their three main attacks: "You're corrupt, mean, or stupid!"

20. Primary liberal "success"—convincing Americans that the Constitution does not limit the government in ways the words clearly state!

21. Liberals don't want debate, they want submission, suppression, and conformity.

22. Democrats are not against favoring the few at the expense of the many. They just want to pick and be a part of the few!

23. A defining democrat objective is freeing able-bodied people from the necessity of having to support and take care of themselves!

24. Democrats continue their fight against what they see as the "unfair, unjust, and unequal" notion of "personal responsibility!"

25. Democrat utopia is success without work and wealth paid for by others!

26. Why are the democrats so openly vitriolic and hateful? No strategy, no new ideas, failed programs, and no leadership— hate is all they've got!

27. Liberalism is not whether you win or lose, but how you place the blame!

28. Liberals disparage free market capitalism, primarily because it does not reward freeloaders!

29. Have you noticed liberals refuse to share their model of what their utopian world would look like if they were successful at enacting all their wishes?

30. Two core democrat categories: Those who give away "free" stuff to stay in power and those who sell their votes to get free stuff!

31. If liberals had great answers, they would be conservatives!

32. Liberalism is the politics of personal destruction! If liberals can't win, they will lie and demonize! They are paid to attack!

33. The most important elements of liberal initiatives are confiscation, coercion, and deception!

34. Detroit provides a future look at the whole US, if liberal spending policies are left in place.

35. When liberals wake up in the morning, their first instinct is to look for something to deplore!

36. The only difference between a parasite and a liberal is the spelling!

37. Picture America with no strong defense, no armed citizenry, no guns, no police, no free markets, killing babies born alive, no healthcare, no border security, huge debts, and no energy—democrats do!

38. Liberals not only want other people's money, they want to run other people's lives!

39. It is truly astonishing how many liberals do not believe in personal responsibility.

40. When is the last time you heard a democrat praise America, a successful business, or free market capitalism? I can't recall either!

38

Free Marxist Capitalism

The most important single central fact about a free market is that no exchange takes place unless both parties benefit.
—Milton Friedman

1. If the rich didn't create all the wealth through free market capitalism, who would they take it from?

2. Without capitalism, how would anticapitalist liberals pay for infrastructure and the safety net?

3. How did so many liberals get rich decrying the evils of free market capitalism?

4. The liberal rap against capitalism is it doesn't allow everyone to win! The conservative rap against big government is it allows only the government to win!

5. We have to make the left start defending socialism instead of us defending liberty.

6. Have you heard a democrat explain how your neighbor making more money than you (income inequality) hurts you in any way!

7. If you prefer the equal sharing of socialist miseries to the unequal sharing of capitalist blessings, you might be a liberal!

8. Apparently, democrats require a bit more study. How does getting rich by selling innovative products hurt the poor?

9. Capitalism is the most powerful engine for prosperity in the history of humankind. Tell a liberal!

10. Competition is anathema to the left because it creates winners/losers.

11. Liberals complain about free markets precisely because free markets diminish central control and protect against coercion!

12. Who is leading toward greater liberty or toward more government control?

13. Free markets rely on incentives and opportunities. Government programs rely on creating faux victims, coercion, and dependency!

14. Free markets are moved by millions of independent transactions. Elitist central planners move government programs!

15. Free markets are driven by consumer preferences and economic self-interest. Politics and political connections drive government programs!

16. Free markets measure and reward success. Government programs measure and reward loyalty to the party, political donors, and voting blocs!

17. To get ahead in the free market system, entrepreneurs need to satisfy willing customers, as opposed to government elites and central planners!

18. Fairness in free markets is determined by millions of everyday citizens. Fairness in government is determined by the special interests with money!

19. In a free market, proper regulation focuses on equal opportunity and fair play. In government-run markets, excessive regulations try to control outcomes!

20. The bureaucratic rules of government work are anathema to innovation and free enterprise!

21. The profit motive breeds the innovation essential for sustained prosperity. Excessive government restrictions breed the opposite!

22. An entrepreneurial culture can lead, whereas a community organizing culture can only agitate, demonize, and divide!

23. An entrepreneurial culture creates earned prosperity; a community-organizing culture redistributes it to those it favors!

24. Do democrats actually know that when we don't have free market capitalism, we get government central planners?

25. No matter the circumstances, Americans will still choose free enterprise over regulation and limited government over statism!

26. Free market capitalism (which democrats hate) looks highly flawed, except when we compare it to every other economic system!

39

The Individual, Ultimate Minority

We've got to do a better job of getting across that America is freedom . . . And freedom is special . . . it needs [protection].
—**Ronald Reagan**

1. As conservatives, we don't believe in the principles of free market capitalism, limited government, and strong defense because they *sound* good, but because they *work*!

2. Conservatives are not against all government; they are against excessive, intrusive, corrupt, and ineffective government!

3. The conservative concept is simple. Help the truly poor and needy and create the opportunity for the rest to go back to work!

4. Conservatives are 100 percent for a safety net that gives the poor and needy a helping hand, but they are against helping freeloaders!

5. Limited government is not just a conservative slogan. It was born as an escape from tyranny and despotism. This must be taught!

6. The first principles offered by our founders brought us prosperity and strength. They can do it again if we get back and stay on the path. Vote!

7. Our founding principles for the past one hundred years have been quietly ignored, ruthlessly thrown aside, and grossly misinterpreted!

8. When founding principles are ignored, unalienable rights are at risk!

9. The natural state of humans is to be free to pursue opportunity. The natural state of liberalism is to take that freedom!

10. Individual liberty is the most radical idea that humans have ever come up with. The natural state of humans is subjugation and tyranny.

11. Conservatism was not made out of thin air. It is rooted in freedom, compassion and justice for all and freedom never goes out of style!

12. Freedom is not just a utopian dream—it is a necessary ingredient in the recipe of American hope, motivation and prosperity!

13. Profit is not just motivation to do better—it funds the safety net for our needy, our lifestyle, and the defense of our country!

14. Free market capitalism is not just an abstract economic system—it is the economic engine that provided unlimited, equal opportunity for all!

15. If we want to see what central planning gets us, have a look at what's left of the USSR.

16. Freedom is difficult to get and harder to keep.

17. You are either *for* the Constitution or you are not! You are for freedom, free markets, rule of law, justice, and equal rights *for all*—or you are not!

18. Let our nation succeed or stumble with our values, our principles, and our way of life! Choose the American way.

19. Pray. Vote Republican and buy a gun.

20. Live free or die.

21. Vote freedom—not government.

40

American Exceptionalism

America is exceptional.
—Jill Burcham

1. America is exceptional! Period!

2. It seems odd to me that so many liberals (including our president) oppose the concept of American exceptionalism.

3. America occupies a special place among nations in part because of its unique history, economic and political opportunities.

4. America occupies a special place among nations in part because of its rejection of a ruling elite and its individual liberties.

5. America occupies a special place among nations in part because of its equal treatment under the law and freedom of religion.

6. America is exceptional in part because of its support for free market capitalism, and its constitutional republic form of government.

7. The concept of American exceptionalism does not mean that America has no flaws or that America has made no mistakes.

8. American exceptionalism does not imply that America should be judged by double standards.

9. American exceptionalism does not imply that Americans are necessarily more capable than others.

10. America stands for a unique set of ideals and principles.

11. American's belief in freedom, self-evident truths, and unalienable rights sets it apart from other nations

12. America is still exceptional even though President Obama and his minions worked hard to make it less so!

13. America became exceptional by virtue of its founding principles that were an exception to the way people had been treated throughout history.

14. American exceptionalism is the concept that human rights and freedom come from God and not government.

15. America is exceptional because its government was established by the people to guarantee and to protect the rights of its citizens.

16. America is exceptional in part because we have universal rights not based on economic or ruling class, religion, or ethnicity!

17. America is great, not by ruling mightily by the sword: but by spreading liberty, guaranteeing individual rights, throwing out the elites and treating all people as equals and supporting capitalism.

18. The first principles offered by our founders brought us prosperity and strength. They can do it again if we get back on the path.

19. The solution to our American problems is to follow the American way—freedom, limited government, and capitalism led by entrepreneurs, not government!

20. For the past one hundred years, our founding principles have been quietly ignored, purposefully misinterpreted, and ruthlessly thrown aside!

21. Our country was founded on the principles of religious freedom and the freedom to be protected from an over-reaching government!

22. Let our nation succeed or stumble with our values, our principles, and our way of life! Choose the American way.

23. Limited government is not just a conservative slogan—it was born as an escape from tyranny and despotism. This must be taught!

24. Freedom is not just a utopian dream. It is a necessary ingredient in the recipe of American hope, motivation, and prosperity!

25. Prosperity is not just an aspiration to do better. It funds the safety net for our needy, our lifestyle, and the defense of our country!

26. In the democrats' world, there is no American exceptionalism, and to the degree they find some, they want to crush it!

27. We are a constitutional republic where God-given rights are protected by laws, not a democracy with mob rule.

28. Government does not give us rights; it protects our rights, even from government intrusion!

29. Every year, we celebrate July 4 because it is the birthday of the US—the day Americans chose to be a free nation.

30. On July 4, 1776, other countries were based on nationality, religion, or ethnicity, but America was created by a set of ideas: freedom, God, family, and e pluribus unum (Latin meaning out of many, one).

31. We have freedom and liberty to pursue our dreams of happiness as hard as we can work.

32. We put trust in God that our rights and liberties come from God. Therefore, they cannot be taken away.

33. Our country is a melting pot of every race, religion, and culture—e pluribus unum (out of many, one).

34. America is *still* exceptional, even if liberals are working hard to make it less so!

35. The trail to American peace and prosperity was clearly marked by our founders in the form of individual rights, maximum personal liberties, and limited governance.

36. No damage has been inflicted on our country or our way of life that cannot be repaired with personal education, broad participation in the political system, and moral character.

37. The strength of our country resides in the minds of our children, and the future of our country will be found in their actions.

38. American revolutionaries shouted, "Don't tread on me!" and "Give me liberty or give me death!"

39. America's great experiment wanted to erase nepotism, tribalism, cronyism, or aristocratic privilege and replace it with meritocracy!

40. America is the only nation, even today, that trusts the *individual* rather than the statists in government. This makes America exceptional!

41. The founders of America created a framework of government to keep government inside. It's the US Constitution!

42. What makes America exceptional is our dedication to the self-evident truth that we are all created equal.

43. America is exceptional, in part because we have universal rights not based on economic or ruling class, religion, or ethnicity!

44. Wouldn't it be great if an American leader would build his or her campaign on the positive elements of American exceptionalism?

45. America defines its notion of American exceptionalism on its history and commitment to equality and liberty for all!

46. What makes America exceptional is our equal rights to life, liberty, and the pursuit of happiness. That means opportunity, no matter what a liberal says!

47. The US motto is e pluribus unum. The motto mandates we stop categorizing other citizens based on race and birth! No more hyphens. We are all free individuals—Americans.

48. The end of American exceptionalism will come only if we become like most places around the world.

49. The Constitution and the Declaration of Independence are so crowded with extraordinary ideas, liberals can't destroy them all at once!

50. Show me a more just society than America. What liberals want is to keep spending other people's money for what they deem to be just.

51. We must remind ourselves why America is exceptional and teach our kids to keep it that way.

52. The end of American exceptionalism will come only if we become like most places the world over—no freedom!

53. Pray. Vote. Buy a gun.

Call to Action: Election Advice

1. Every day I am asked why I work so hard with tweets, speeches, and my books to present my view of the American way. Answer—It's my job.

2. It's our job as citizens and parents to engage in how we are being governed and to help inform and educate others to understand what is at risk.

3. It's our job to make sure we have a strong defense, excellent education, and equal opportunity for all.

4. It's our job to keep government limited to that which only government can do.

5. It's our job because the US Constitution makes it our job, and if we don't do it, others might do it wrong.

6. It's our job to promote personal responsibility while we help those truly in need.

7. It's our job to teach our children our founding principles so they will be ready to take over when it's their turn.

8. It's our job to teach others why and how America is exceptional.

9. It's our job to preserve that for which our founders fought and died to give us.

10. It's our job to leave a better and safer land for our kids than what it is today. This cannot be left to politicians, bureaucrats, or judges.

11. It's our job to be good parents and good Americans.

    - Right is right; wrong is wrong.

    - American exceptionalism is real.

    - Educate and engage.

    - Children, patriotism, and optimism.

    - The constitution is a contract between our government and its citizens.

    - It is worth our effort to preserve that which our founders gave us.

    - The philosophy of common sense conservatism can and will prevail.

    - No one is an angel, and it is never an angel we send to Washington.

- Organize your thoughts and develop your own set of principles.

- Think for yourself and determine your own course of action.

- We care; we are smart. We can, and will, do this job right.

- America's people are strong, and America's future remains bright. Our children deserve it!

Pray. Buy a Gun. Vote Republican.